DATE DUE

BRODART, CO.   Cat. No. 23-221-003

Nathaniel Hawthorne's
THE
SCARLET
LETTER

Bloom's
NOTES

A CONTEMPORARY
LITERARY VIEWS BOOK

Edited and with an Introduction by
HAROLD BLOOM

3 5 7 9 8 6 4

Library of Congress Cataloging-in-Publication Data
Nathaniel Hawthorne's The scarlet letter / edited and with an introduction by Harold Bloom.
p.   cm.—(Contemporary literary views)
"Books by Nathaniel Hawthorne":
Includes bibliographical references.
ISBN 0-7910-3650-2
1. Hawthorne, Nathaniel, 1804–1864. Scarlet letter.
2. Historical fiction, American History and criticism. 3. Mothers and daughters in literature. 4. Massachusetts—In literature. 5. Puritans in literature. 6. Adultery in literature. 7. Women in literature. I. Bloom, Harold. II. Series: Bloom, Harold. Contemporary literary views.
PS1868.N38 1996
813'.3—dc20
95-12184
CIP

Contents

User's Guide

THIS VOLUME is designed to present biographical, critical, and bibliographical information on Nathaniel Hawthorne and *The Scarlet Letter*. Following Harold Bloom's introduction, there appears a detailed biography of the author, discussing the major events in his life and his important literary works. Then follows a thematic and structural analysis of the work, in which significant themes, patterns, and motifs are traced. An annotated list of characters supplies brief information on the chief characters in the work.

A selection of critical extracts, derived from previously published material by leading critics, then follows. The extracts consist of statements by the author on his work, early reviews of the work, and later evaluations down to the present day. The items are arranged chronologically by date of first publication. A bibliography of Hawthorne's writings (including a complete listing of all books he wrote, cowrote, edited, and translated in his lifetime, and important posthumous publications), a list of additional books and articles on him and on *The Scarlet Letter,* and an index of themes conclude the volume.

Introduction

HAROLD BLOOM

The Western authorities on a nearly universal malady, sexual jealousy, are Shakespeare, Hawthorne, Freud, and Proust. *The Scarlet Letter,* one of the double handful of great American novels, is in some of its aspects untouched by the madness of jealousy, despite its pervasive theme of adultery. Only when Roger Chillingworth is the focus does Hawthorne's prose-romance take on the dissonances that recall Shakespeare's *Othello* and *The Winter's Tale,* and that prophesy Freud's and Proust's analyses of jealous obsessiveness. Chillingworth is both a devil and an avenging angel, at once sadist and masochist, not only ambiguous in his own nature but extraordinarily ambivalent toward the Reverend Mr. Dimmesdale, his timid and equivocal usurper. Dimmesdale and Chillingworth are one another's victims, and yet each needs the other in order to go on living. The reader is likely to note that Chillingworth frequently seems more a portrait of Satan than of a seventeenth-century scholar-physician. In some ways the cuckolded husband of Hester Prynne is as occult a figure as Pearl—the faery-child of Hester and Dimmesdale—or Mistress Hibbins the witch. Much of what we think of as human psychology seems as irrelevant to Chillingworth as it does to Pearl and Mistress Hibbins. And yet the psychology of sexual jealousy is very relevant to Chillingworth: it helps illuminate the strangeness of his conduct, toward Dimmesdale in particular. The Shakespearean version of sexual jealousy—essentially inherited by all subsequent authors—is transmuted by Milton's Satan before it reaches Chillingworth. Something of the aura of Satan playing Peeping Tom as he spies upon Adam and Eve still lingers as Chillingworth contemplates Hester and Dimmesdale. But the archetype remains Shakespeare's Iago, conniving the destruction of Othello and Desdemona in order to enhance his own sense of self, or what Milton's Satan called his "sense of injured merit."

Sexual jealousy as a sense of injured merit may, in the last analysis, be the fear that there will not be enough space or enough time for oneself. In Chillingworth's instance, the extended interval that he seeks might be interpreted as the sadist's desire to prolong his satisfaction at his victim's torments, yet that would be inadequate to the complexity of Hawthorne's art. When Chillingworth desperately attempts to prevent Dimmesdale from pronouncing his revelation of guilt, we hear a multitude of motives mingling together:

> "Madman, hold! What is your purpose?" whispered he. "Wave back that woman! Cast off this child! All shall be well! Do not blacken your fame, and perish in dishonor! I can yet save you! Would you bring infamy on your sacred profession?"

We may doubt Chillingworth's concern for the good name of the clergy, but he certainly does have a considerable psychic investment both in the survival and in the reputation of Dimmesdale. For artistic reasons that have to do with preserving the romance element in *The Scarlet Letter,* Hawthorne does not allow himself, or us, an acute psychological analysis of Chillingworth (or of Pearl or Mistress Hibbins). If you do the devil's work, then you become the devil, and so we have the oddity that Iago and Chillingworth become considerably more diabolic than Milton's Satan ever manages to become, despite his titanic efforts. Chillingworth quite forgets he is a man, and becomes an incarnate jealousy instead. His pride in keeping Dimmesdale alive is augmented by the clergyman's public image of holiness, while Chillingworth's deepest pleasure resides in the conviction that Dimmesdale ultimately will share in the physician's spiritual damnation, linked for eternity by their roles in Hester's tragic story.

Dimmesdale, caught between Hester and Chillingworth, has neither the blessed strength of Hester's balked capacity for life nor the infernal strength of Chillingworth's impotent hatred for life. The minister's character and personality, despite his acute sensibility, render him too weak to be tragic. When we think of *The Scarlet Letter* as a portrait of human character in dramatic conflict with itself, we are compelled to center upon Hester, whose power of endurance is almost frightening in its sustained intensity. Dimmesdale is so pallid in comparison that we wonder how he ever provoked an extraordinary passion in Hester, who is so much superior to him in her capacity for an authentic life. Subtle as Hawthorne is throughout the novel, he is pragmatically sinuous in finding a multitude of ways to persuade us of Hester's sexual power. When he speculates that, but for Pearl, Hester would have been a second Ann Hutchinson, a major religious rebel against seventeenth-century American Puritanism, he associates his heroine with a violent energy, "the flesh and blood of action," that can only be sexual. Then *The Scarlet Letter* would have been a realistic tragedy, since Hester in full rebellion would have become a prefeminist martyr, immolated by the righteous men of Puritan Boston.

Readers now, as we approach the Millennium, may be tempted to undervalue the courage and physical stamina that Hester manifests in maintaining her seven-year defiance of her entire society: its religion, morality, and sense of election by God and by divinely decreed history. Hawthorne never violates her dignity, her self-reliance, her loyalty to the unworthy Dimmesdale. At least a century ahead of her own time, Hester would be fierce enough to die for her sense of self were it not, as we have seen, for her maternal obligations. Yet she is too large and passionate a being to have any sense of injured merit; within limits she bears her outcast status as the cost of her confirmation as a natural woman, and her consciousness of her own "sin" is highly ambivalent. It is difficult not to feel that Hester Prynne is as much Nathaniel Hawthorne as Emma Bovary is Gustave Flaubert. Hester indeed is a Hawthorne-like artist; her embroidery is a metaphor for her creator's narrative art, and the scarlet letter she wears is defiantly an aesthetic artifact, representing art far more truly than it represents adultery, though hardly in the view of Puritan Boston.

Hawthorne's implicit celebration of Hester's sexual nature is also necessarily a celebration of her highly individual will, which is more a post-Emersonian nineteenth-century version of the Protestant will than it is a Puritan kind of seeing, saying, and acting. A Puritan will could not survive isolation; Hester's will belongs to a different order of American spiritual consciousness, one that can find freedom in solitude, even when that solitude is a punishment imposed by a repressive society. Hawthorne informs us that the scarlet letter has "the effect of a spell, taking her out of the ordinary relations with humanity, and enclosing her in a sphere by herself." Since the Puritan public sphere is marked by sadism, hypocrisy, and (as portrayed by Hawthorne with particular skill) a shocking lack of compassion, we can wonder why Hester does not take Pearl and depart into what might be a wholesome exile. The answer, as Hawthorne intimates, is deeply pathetic: having chosen Dimmesdale, Hester refuses to abandon what she regards as her true marriage. When he dies, his head supported by her bosom, he is still totally unworthy of her, and yet she has remained true to the integrity of her own will. ✤

Biography of Nathaniel Hawthorne

Nathaniel Hawthorne was born in Salem, Massachusetts, on July 4, 1804; he was descended on both sides from prominent New England Puritans, including Judge John Hathorne (the older spelling of the name), one of the most notorious of the Salem witchcraft judges of 1692. In 1809, after the death of his father, Hawthorne, his mother, and his two sisters lived at the home of his maternal grandparents. After studying at Samuel Archer's School (1819), Hawthorne attended Bowdoin College in Brunswick, Maine (1821–25), where his classmates included the poet Henry Wadsworth Longfellow and Franklin Pierce, later the 14th president of the United States, whose biography Hawthorne would write. In 1825 Hawthorne returned to Salem to live with his mother.

Rather than entering a trade or profession as he was expected to do, Hawthorne spent the next dozen years or so in relative isolation, concentrating on reading and writing. In 1828, anonymously and at his own expense, he published a novel, *Fanshawe,* which drew heavily upon his experiences at Bowdoin. He later withdrew the book and destroyed every copy he could find. Between 1830 and 1837 Hawthorne wrote tales and sketches for various periodicals (notably S. G. Goodrich's annual, *The Token*), and in 1837 a collection was published as *Twice-Told Tales;* an expanded edition appeared in 1842. After becoming engaged to Sophia Peabody in 1839, Hawthorne took a job as a measurer in the Boston custom house (1839–40), and in 1841 joined the Brook Farm community in West Roxbury, Massachusetts; but he withdrew from this utopian community (which was run by the Transcendentalists, who preached simple living and high moral ideals) after several months. In 1842 Hawthorne and Sophia were married; they settled in Concord, where Hawthorne became part of the circle that included such writers as Ralph Waldo Emerson, Henry David Thoreau, Margaret Fuller, and A. Bronson Alcott.

In 1841 Hawthorne issued a three-volume children's history of New England under the generic title *Grandfather's Chair.* In 1846, the year his son Julian was born, appeared *Mosses from an Old Manse,* a collection of sketches and tales reprinted from various periodicals. Between 1846 and 1849 he worked as a surveyor in the Salem custom house, and in 1850 he published *The Scarlet Letter,* which won him considerable fame. Although it is now considered a classic novel, Hawthorne was careful to subtitle this work as a "romance," suggesting a looser structure than the novel and a freer use of fantasy, melodrama, and symbolism instead of unadorned realism. *The Scarlet Letter* is set in seventeenth-century New England, and Hawthorne sought to explore the Puritan conscience through a drama of adultery and revenge.

During 1850 and 1851 Hawthorne lived in Lenox, Massachusetts, where he became friendly with Herman Melville. In 1851 his second daughter, Rose, was born (Una, the first, had been born in 1844), and that same year *The House of the Seven Gables* (also subtitled a "romance") was published; this tale of ancestral guilt was partially based on Hawthorne's own family history. Also in 1851 appeared a third collection of shorter pieces, *The Snow-Image and Other Twice-Told Tales. The Blithedale Romance,* based in large part on Hawthorne's experiences at Brook Farm, appeared in 1852, and was followed by two retellings of Greek myths for children, *A Wonder-Book for Girls and Boys* (1852) and *Tanglewood Tales* (1853).

In 1853 Hawthorne was appointed by President Franklin Pierce to serve as United States consul in England; he remained in Liverpool in this position until 1857. He then spent the years 1857–59 living in Rome and Florence, an experience that inspired the novel *The Marble Faun* (1860). This was to be his last completed work of fiction. In 1860 Hawthorne returned to Concord, where he spent the rest of his life; in 1863 he published *Our Old Home,* a series of essays on England and Anglo-American relations.

In 1864 Hawthorne traveled to New Hampshire in an attempt to improve his failing health. On May 19 of that year he died at Plymouth, Massachusetts, leaving unfinished four works of fiction that were ultimately published posthumously: *Septimius Felton; or, The Elixir of Life* (1872), *The Dolliver Romance* (1876), *Doctor Grimshawe's Secret* (1883), and "The Ancestral Footstep" (1883). After his death Sophia Hawthorne edited his English and American notebooks, and his daughter Una edited his French and Italian notebooks. There have also been several collected editions of his letters. A landmark critical edition of his work was published by Ohio State University Press in twenty volumes between 1963 and 1988. ❖

Thematic and
Structural Analysis

The Scarlet Letter begins with a lengthy autobiographical introductory section entitled "The Custom-House." Before launching
into the tale itself, Hawthorne (if indeed the narrator of "The
Custom-House" is Hawthorne) tells the story of how he came
into possession of the materials on which *The Scarlet Letter* is
based. Three years previously, he tells us, having given up trying to make a living as a writer, he had accepted a political
appointment as a "Surveyor of the Revenue" at a custom house
(a place where business relating to shipping is conducted) in
his hometown of Salem, Massachusetts. In wry tones, he
describes the custom house as a place worn by the effects of
time and boredom. He provides gentle satirical sketches of a
variety of decrepit functionaries who pretend to work there,
biding their time until the next meal or mechanically recount-
ing stories of more lively former days. He includes himself in
his mockery as he regrets the "home-feeling" that ties him to
this location of his family's Puritan roots, where the ghosts of
his ancestors still cling to him with "oyster-like tenacity." While
patiently performing the dry tasks required of him at this dreary site, he finds among heaps of discarded business documents
"a certain affair of fine red cloth"—a faded and worn letter "A"
made out of scarlet fabric and embroidered around its edges
with gold stitching. He holds it to his chest and finds to his sur-
prise that it burns him—"as if the letter were not of red cloth,
but of red hot iron." He then unrolls the ancient papers to
which the letter had been attached and finds therein the por-
tentous details of the life of Hester Prynne.

While it is extraneous to the main plot, the "Custom-House"
preface establishes a number of the principal thematic concerns
in *The Scarlet Letter.* Primary among these are what one might
call the burden of history and, more simply, guilt. By speaking
regretfully of his own family's ancient ties to Salem, by sketch-
ing a variety of aging local characters all more or less trapped
in their youth, by evoking a general atmosphere of moldiness
and decay, and by representing his own impulse to write as

the response to the command of a deceased historian's ghost, the preface foreshadows the novel's general insistence on the power of the past over the present. The inescapability of the past is one of the most important lessons that Hester, the Reverend Arthur Dimmesdale, and the reader will learn over the course of the novel. The emotion of guilt, Hawthorne implies, exists to teach the heart this truth.

The first chapter of the story proper is entirely devoted to the presentation of two symbols. Before introducing us to any of the characters or narrating any event of the plot, Hawthorne shows us two simple images—a prison door and a wild rose-bush, around which are gathered a group of men and women in Puritan dress. These two symbols may be said to represent the two great impersonal forces that come into conflict in the novel. Principally, the rosebush stands for the spontaneous and irrepressible life of nature and instinct, while the prison door stands for the harsh limitations that must be imposed on nature to maintain order in human societies. It is characteristic of Hawthorne to present his themes by means of such concrete and richly evocative images. The novel is full of them—from the scarlet letter itself, to the clothing of Pearl, to the minister's hand over his heart. It is also characteristic of Hawthorne frequently to suggest a variety of ways in which these images may be interpreted, but to leave the final determination of their significance up to the reader.

The prison door opens in the second chapter, and the novel's heroine emerges. Hester Prynne is described as strikingly beautiful, with lustrous and luxurious red-brown hair and an elegant, even haughty manner. But her proud bearing cannot hide the two marks of shame she carries with her—a three-month-old baby girl who was born in prison, and a large crimson letter "A." She ascends the "pillory"—a "gallows-like" platform on which guilty criminals were exposed to public ridicule. Forced to endure the taunts of a scandalized and resentful Puritan community, Hester retreats into memories of her father and her husband and the European city where they had planned to live. Feelings of immense pain, loneliness, and near-madness grip Hester's mind as she confronts the full harshness of her situation.

In the third chapter Hester is startled out of her anguished reverie by the sight of her long-absent husband's "pale scholar-like visage" among the staring faces of the crowd. His pained look reveals that he has grasped something of what has happened, but he signals to Hester not to reveal his presence. Under the cover of anonymity he inquires among the people in the crowd as to the story of the woman on the scaffold. From them he and the reader learn that Hester had been sent ahead to Boston by her husband in Amsterdam. After hearing "no tidings" of him for two years, we are told, Hester committed the adulterous act for which she is now being punished. She deserved death according to the community's rules, the people in the crowd grumble, but the young minister—Dimmesdale—intervened mercifully on her behalf. Still concealing his identity, the anonymous stranger admits that it "irks" him that the man who shared her sin refuses to share her punishment, and he vows ominously that the identity of the fellow sinner "will be known." Chapter three ends with Hester steadfastly refusing to succumb to the young minister's public exhortations that she reveal the identity of her fellow sinner. Her responses testify to the depth of her love and loyalty: "Would that I might endure his agony," she says, "as well as my own."

In chapter four Hester's husband gains access to Hester by offering his services as a physician. Finally supplying his name, Roger Chillingworth, he is allowed temporarily to take up residence in the prison to attend to the "half-frenzied" prisoners. From his conversations with Hester, we learn that their marriage had been loveless. Chillingworth had hoped that Hester's youthful presence would assuage an aging spirit dried up by excessive absorption in researches in alchemy (the search for the "elixir of life," or the substance that would transmute base metals into gold), but Hester reminds him that she neither felt nor feigned any love for him. He accepts that he thus bears some responsibility for her defection, but he insists nonetheless that she must reveal the identity of him who "has wronged us both." She refuses to tell him, but she does promise to keep Chillingworth's identity a secret—a promise she quickly begins to regret. "Hast thou enticed me," she wonders as

Chillingworth leaves the prison, "into a bond that will prove the ruin of my soul?" The bond proves, at any rate, a critical link in the plot.

The next two chapters are largely devoted to descriptions of the extraordinary character of Hester Prynne and her daughter, Pearl. Wearing the scarlet letter always on her breast, Hester takes up a spare and lonely existence in a thatched cottage on the outskirts of town. With only Pearl for company, she dresses herself coarsely and bears patiently the taunts of the local children and the reprimands of the elders. The only outlet for her sorrows is the needlework by which she makes her modest living. In contrast to the stark plainness of her own garb, she produces elegant and sumptuous handiwork for her daughter and for the members of the community. Her work is greatly admired and becomes fashionable—gorgeously adorning the town's various legal, religious, and political ceremonies. She gives the extra money she makes from sewing to charities or to the needy cases who increasingly seek her out for solace and guidance. And perhaps most remarkably, she never attempts to leave Salem.

Why, the narrator speculates, does Hester never take the opportunity to flee into the surrounding wilderness or take ship back to Europe? Part of the answer is her loyalty to her fellow sinner—Dimmesdale. But the rest of the answer points to one of the novel's more important and more subtle themes. Hester's attitude toward law is more complex than simple defiance. She is not presented merely as the victim of an unduly harsh legal code. Hester stays in Salem in part because she genuinely wishes to atone for her sin. Part of her continues to believe that submission to the community's law holds the possibility of redemption—that "the torture of her daily shame would thereby purge her soul, and work out another purity than that which she had lost." Whether or not she achieves such ultimate purification, there is no question that by courageously facing up to her ordeal she does strengthen and enhance her moral awareness. She develops, for example, prescient insight into the "hidden sin in other hearts," and she comes to feel sincere compassion for the weak, the poor, and the outcast.

Pearl's attitude toward the law is not so complex as Hester's. From the moment after her birth when she fixes her gaze upon the scarlet letter, she remains entirely defiant, capricious, and ungovernable. She is described as somehow nonhuman, or elflike. Her moods and gestures are sudden, uncanny, and impulsive. Hawthorne takes every opportunity to place her in close association with nature and natural creatures. We are meant, in short, to take her as representative of the wild, natural, prerational side of human society—the purely impulsive part of the self that refuses to submit to all "civilizing" constraints. Hester quickly learns not to try to control Pearl, but Pearl's waywardness never ceases to worry her.

Hester's worst fears for her daughter are nearly realized in chapters seven and eight. Two or three years having passed since her emergence from prison, Hester hears rumors that the magistrates are planning to take Pearl away on the grounds that she is a "demon-child" from whom her mother must be protected. She goes to speak to Governor Bellingham about this matter and finds it to be true. The novel's general preoccupation with the conflict between authority and freedom is refigured as Pearl misbehaves in the governor's mansion. Her odd mannerisms and her mischievous answers to the governor's questions about the basics of Puritan theology confirm his worst suspicions. It is only Hester's shrieks of protest and Dimmesdale's intercession at the last moment that prevent the governor from taking Pearl away. Pearl tenderly touches Dimmesdale's cheek in gratitude for his help. Chillingworth is also on the scene, and he notes that the minister speaks with "a strange earnestness" in defending the sacredness of the bond between Hester and her child.

Goaded by this and other hints, Chillingworth now begins a relentless and remorseless probing of Dimmesdale's heart and spirit. For the next four chapters, the focus turns to Chillingworth's demonic effort to determine Dimmesdale's involvement in Hester's crime. Exemplary in the outward forms of religious life, Chillingworth professes admiration for the eloquent and pious Dimmesdale and takes him for his spiritual guide. At the same time, Dimmesdale's health begins to fail; he seems frail and thin and continually puts his hand wearily over his heart. The people of the town appeal to Chillingworth to bring his medical expertise to the beloved young minister's aid, and the "leech" gladly complies—even arranging to have himself lodged in the same house so that he can watch over Dimmesdale more closely. Here, like a spiritual parasite, Chillingworth burrows into Dimmesdale's soul—embroiling him at every opportunity in painstaking discussions of sin and guilt, and tirelessly questioning him about the Hester Prynne case. Chillingworth arrives at his diagnosis, informing Dimmesdale that his spirit and body are so intermingled that he must disburden himself of his spiritual ills before his body can recover. Dimmesdale rejects this advice, insisting that he will confess only to God, but Chillingworth's suspicions are only sharpened. One night after Dimmesdale has fallen into a deep slumber, Chillingworth thrusts his vestments aside and sees something extraordinary that throws him into a "ghastly rapture." A letter "A" has been seared into the minister's very flesh.

Chillingworth's discovery only increases his desire to exact "intimate revenge" on Dimmesdale, and he sets about doing so. As Chillingworth's insidious assault intensifies, however, Dimmesdale's standing in the eyes of the community ascends ever higher. The anguish of his own guilt has given Dimmesdale's preaching unusual emotional range and breadth, and his parishioners take his frequent verbal self-abasement as a sign of exceptional humility. Meanwhile, in the privacy of his chambers at night Dimmesdale fasts until he is weak, and he beats himself with a bloody scourge. On one such night he goes to the public square and ascends the scaffold. He shrieks aloud, and then, envisioning the whole town discovering his pathetic form, bursts into a peal of laughter. But a childish laugh in response reveals that Pearl and Hester are the only witnesses of his strange vigil. They join him on the scaffold, and the three of them hold hands. A meteor passes, and they all perceive an immense letter "A" emblazoned across the sky. In the lingering glow they also perceive the form of Chillingworth standing a small distance from the scaffold. Startled and full of dread, Dimmesdale asks, "Who is he? I hate him." But he is forced to make excuses and go home with the demonic leech when Chillingworth approaches the scaffold and chides Dimmesdale for getting too absorbed in his books. The next day Dimmesdale preaches a discourse that is said to be the best the parishioners have ever heard.

Meanwhile, Hester has resolved to confront Chillingworth about the tormenting of Dimmesdale. Increasingly she has taken on the role of a Sister of Mercy, tending to the needs of the outcast and unfortunate members of the Salem community. Among the poor and weak her "A" has come to stand for "able," in recognition of her patient strength in caring for them. It is in this capacity that she seeks out Chillingworth, her husband, and informs him that she plans to reveal his true identity to Dimmesdale, the father of her child. But Chillingworth's vengeful single-mindedness has by now completely taken control of him, and he refuses to take pity on the minister. The important theme of moral change is thus played out in two opposing directions: the flowering of Hester's moral sensibility is contrasted with the shrinking and narrowing of her husband's spirit.

Soon after speaking with Chillingworth, Hester goes to wait for Dimmesdale on the forest path where she knows he will pass in return from a visit to the Indian converts. Her encounter with him there, as it is described over the next three chapters, is the thematic and structural focal point of the novel. All the book's major conflicts—freedom versus responsibility, future versus past, forgiveness versus guilt, individual versus community, nature versus civilization—are brought to a head as Hester attempts to persuade Dimmesdale that they must leave Salem and start again in the American wilderness or in Europe. "Begin all anew," Hester urges the minister in quintessential American fashion. "Is the world, then, so narrow? Whither leads yon forest-track? . . . Exchange this false life for a true one." A long-unfamiliar joy fills Dimmesdale's heart as he agrees to Hester's plan, and he "feels the excitement of breathing the wild, free atmosphere of an unredeemed, unchristianized, lawless region." Hester is no less relieved and excited; in gestures symbolic of the liberation of her long-suppressed impulsiveness and sensuality, she flings away the scarlet letter and unbinds her luxurious hair. For a moment feelings of hopefulness, freedom, mercy, and natural spontaneity prevail as

Hester and the minister enjoy a perfect exhilaration. But it is characteristic of Hawthorne's psychological realism not to allow such an exalted mood to last for too long. When Hester and the minister try to induce Pearl to come and share their happiness, the child throws a fit and refuses to acknowledge her mother until she readorns herself with the scarlet letter. Hester submits to the child's whim, saying resignedly that she must wear the letter a little while longer in any case, until the ship on which they plan to escape departs for England. A kind of grayness descends upon her as she once again pins the letter on her breast, and Pearl runs to the stream to wash off the minister's kisses.

On his way back into the town, Dimmesdale feels nonetheless rejuvenated and lighthearted. He only barely restrains himself from saying blasphemous things about the communion ritual to a passing deacon, or uttering "naughty" words to a band of Puritan schoolchildren, or joining in the merriment of a drunken sailor. The theme of the human potential for moral change is thus raised again. In this case a radical transformation seems to have come about too suddenly; the formerly sober minister is left disoriented and unbalanced by his suddenly altered perspective. Shocked by his own whims, Dimmesdale hurries into the safety of his study, where he stays and works until daylight on the election day sermon he is scheduled to give on the very day of his planned departure from Salem.

On election day, as Hester mingles with the crowd gathered to celebrate the public holiday, the ship captain informs her to her horror that a close friend of her companion has arranged to sail with them—Roger Chillingworth. It is thus with a sinking heart that she stands outside the church from which she is still excluded and listens to the muffled risings and fallings of Dimmesdale's voice. Even at this distance she discerns the plaintive power of his speaking. When the voice halts and the doors open she is not surprised to hear the churchyard fill with praise for the minister's sermon. He is said to have reached prophetic heights of eloquence, to have predicted a glorious destiny for the Puritan community, but also to have intimated his own approaching death. He appears near physical exhaustion as he emerges from the church, but he manages to stop the procession, call Hester and Pearl to his side, and with their support ascend the nearby scaffold. Assuring the puzzled Hester that this plan is better, that he is dying and has only a short time left in which to admit his shame, he announces his fellowship in sin with Hester to the townsfolk, baring his marked breast. He then sinks dying upon the scaffold, asking God's forgiveness of Chillingworth and thanking God for sending Chillingworth and the scarlet letter to make him and Hester aware of their sin. "Thou hast escaped me," Chillingworth hisses. "God hath proved his mercy most of all," Dimmesdale says in his final words, "in my afflictions."

In conclusion, we are told of the various interpretations the members of the town came to give of the events on the scaffold. We learn also that Chillingworth's vitality ebbed as soon as he was deprived of an object for his consuming hatred: he died within a year, but left a large amount of property in America and in England to Pearl. Neither Pearl nor Hester were seen for some years in New England, but after a time Hester returned, took up residence in her old cottage, and even resumed wearing the scarlet letter. It was believed that she had grandchildren back in Europe because she had been seen knitting infants' garments. She tended kindly to the poor and the sick, counseled women in their struggles, and spoke hopefully of a future time when the relationship between men and women might be established on a more just and loving foundation. Over time, the scarlet letter ceased to be regarded as a stigma and was seen as something "to be sorrowed over," something to behold with "awe" and "reverence."

Such a sober conclusion may seem disheartening when contrasted with the high hopes for a new life Hester expressed to the minister during their encounter in the forest, but it is consistent with Hawthorne's thematic emphasis throughout the novel. From the very beginning, in the "Custom-House" preface, he insists on the difficulty of making a clean break with the past. Just as Hawthorne himself realized that he was inextricably tied to Salem and to the troubled legacy of his Puritan ancestors, Hester and Dimmesdale accept that they cannot simply "start anew"—that their identities are intimately connected with their history and the history of their community. It is possible for Hester to appropriate and transform the identity bequeathed to her by society and convention, but it is not possible for her to reject it outright, however fervently she may wish to do so. She can embroider the scarlet letter with gold thread, she can change what it stands for from "adulteress" to "able" or "angel," but she cannot dispense with it altogether. Similarly, it is only when Dimmesdale admits his sin to the community he loves that he is freed from Chillingworth's torture. Hawthorne thus perhaps attempts to provide some corrective to the American confidence in the radical freedom of the individual to sever the bonds of community and reinvent himself or herself entirely anew. The forest encounter between Hester and Dimmesdale acknowledges the powerful allure of such freedom, but the rest of the novel suggests that it is an illusion. ✤

—*Neal Dolan*
Harvard University

List of Characters

Hester Prynne is the heroine of *The Scarlet Letter.* She is presented as a flawed but richly complex and ultimately greatly admirable personality. She is a strikingly beautiful woman, and the sensual and passionate side of her character comes into conflict with the moral strictness of Puritan culture. When she becomes pregnant while her husband is still in Europe, she is forced to wear the scarlet letter "A" (for "adulteress") on her breast, thus becoming an outcast and a pariah to her community. But she shows a remarkable capacity to adapt and learn from her cruel situation. She makes herself indispensable to the community by providing it with gorgeous needlework, and she takes pity on the sick and the needy. She bears up under the taunts of children and the lectures of ministers, tenderly caring for her daughter and stubbornly refusing to give the name of her adulterous lover, even while he hypocritically lectures her in public. Her repentance for her sin is as sincere as the love that drove her to it. Over the course of the novel her remarkable capacities for compassion, humility, devotion, loyalty, and perseverance transform her from moral outcast to moral exemplar and prophet.

The Reverend Arthur Dimmesdale is Hester Prynne's counterpart. He is a young minister of great learning, sincere piety, and formidable eloquence, but his single departure from the straight and narrow path of virtue brings about tragic consequences. He impregnates Hester Prynne, and she is punished fiercely as an adulterer. Believing at first that to admit his fellowship in sin with Hester would deprive him of all capacity to do further good in the community, he does not admit his complicity. Universally admired and looked up to as a moral authority, he finds himself in an excruciatingly hypocritical position. At one point he even exhorts Hester in public to reveal the identity of her fellow sinner—knowing that she will not because it is himself, and she is too pure of heart to wish to see him suffer. He scourges himself in private out of guilt for his hypocrisy. His situation is made the more painful by the remorseless efforts of Roger Chillingworth, Hester's husband, to determine his guilt and to take revenge upon him. He is eventually driven to mental exhaustion and an early death by these unbearable strains. But he does manage to confess his guilt to the community before he dies. One is left with the impression of a very good, very intelligent, but—compared with Hester—relatively weak man.

Pearl is Hester's and Dimmesdale's daughter. Impulsive, uncanny, and ungovernable, she is a symbol of natural instinct and intuition. At one point, the elders of Salem try to take her away from Hester because they think that she is a "demon-child." For Hawthorne, she is less a demon than a kind of Romantic nature-spirit. In the most overtly Romantic passages in the novel, she is shown cavorting in nature and communing with wild animals.

Roger Chillingworth is Hester's husband. A dry scholar obsessed with alchemy and considerably older than Hester, he was attracted by her youth and beauty. They were married in Amsterdam two years before the action of the novel starts. After sending Hester ahead to America to prepare things for his arrival, he arrives two years later to find Hester on the pillory being punished for adultery. His entire personality is soon taken over by a demonic drive for revenge against her lover. Guessing correctly that Dimmesdale is the culprit, he pursues him mercilessly, driving him to an early grave. He is a study in the power of obsessive rationality to narrow and dehumanize the human personality. He commits what Hawthorne deems the worst of sins by "violating the sanctity of a human heart" in his torment of Dimmesdale. His only affirmative gesture is to leave Pearl property in Europe and America when he dies. ❖

Critical Views

[Hawthorne's most significant statement about *The Scarlet Letter* is found in his introduction, "The Custom-House," which appears in most editions of the novel. In letters he wrote while writing the work, Hawthorne worried that the book was too uniformly somber to be pleasing to the general public.]

My book, the publisher tells me, will not be out before April. He speaks of it in tremendous terms of approbation; so does Mrs. Hawthorne, to whom I read the conclusion, last night. It broke her heart and sent her to bed with a grievous headache—which I look upon as triumphant success! Judging from its effect on her and the publisher, I may calculate on what bowlers call a 'ten-strike.' Yet I do not make any such calculation. Some portions of the book are powerfully written; but my writings do not, nor ever will, appeal to the broadest class of sympathies, and therefore will not attain a very wide popularity. Some like them very much; others care nothing for them, and see nothing in them. There is an introduction to this book—giving a sketch of my Custom-House life, with an imaginative touch here and there—which perhaps may be more widely attractive than the main narrative. The latter lacks sunshine. To tell you the truth it is—(I hope Mrs. Bridge is not present)—it is positively a h–ll-fired story, into which I found it almost impossible to throw any cheering light.

> —Nathaniel Hawthorne, Letter to Horatio Bridge (February 4, 1850), *Letters 1843–1853*, ed. Thomas Woodson, L. Neal Smith, and Norman Holmes Pearson (Columbus: Ohio State University Press, 1985), pp. 311–12

ARTHUR CLEVELAND COXE ON THE MORALITY OF *THE SCARLET LETTER*

[Arthur Cleveland Coxe (1818–1896) was an American theologian, poet, and critic in the later nineteenth century. Among his important books are *Christian Ballads* (1840) and *Halloween: A Romaunt* (1842). This review of *The Scarlet Letter* exemplifies the degree to which religious and moral concerns colored the evaluation of a literary work in this period. Coxe is particularly concerned with the effect of the book upon "Christian maidens," and he believes that the book—though outwardly pure in its language—is profoundly immoral for its apparent condoning of adultery.]

Why has our author selected such a theme? Why, amid all the suggestive incidents of life in a wilderness; of a retreat from civilization to which, in every individual case, a thousand circumstances must have concurred to reconcile human nature with estrangement from home and country; or amid the historical connections of our history with Jesuit adventure, savage invasion, regicide outlawry, and French aggression, should the taste of Mr. Hawthorne have preferred as the proper material for romance, the nauseous amour of a Puritan pastor, with a frail creature of his charge, whose mind is represented as far more debauched than her body? Is it, in short, because a running undertide of filth has become as requisite to a romance, as death in the fifth act to a tragedy? Is the French era actually begun in our literature? And is the flesh, as well as the world and the devil, to be henceforth dished up in fashionable novels, and discussed at parties, by spinsters and their beaux, with as unconcealed a relish as they give to the vanilla in their ice cream? We would be slow to believe it, and we hope our author would not willingly have it so, yet we honestly believe that *The Scarlet Letter* has already done not a little to degrade our literature, and to encourage social licentiousness: it has started other pens on like enterprises, and has loosed the restraint of many tongues, that have made it an apology for "the evil communications which corrupt good manners." We are painfully tempted to believe that it is a book made for the market, and that the market has made it merchantable, as they do game, by letting everybody understand that the commodity is in high condition, and smells strongly of incipient putrefaction.

We shall entirely mislead our reader if we give him to suppose that *The Scarlet Letter* is coarse in its details, or indecent in its phraseology. This very article of our own, is far less suited to ears polite, than any page of the romance before us; and the reason is, we call things by their right names, while the romance never hints the shocking words that belong to its things, but, like Mephistopheles, insinuates that the arch-fiend himself is a very tolerable sort of person, if nobody would call him Mr. Devil. We have heard of persons who could not bear the reading of some Old Testament Lessons in the service of the Church: such persons would be delighted with our author's story; and damsels who shrink at the reading of the Decalogue, would probably luxuriate in bathing their imagination in the crystal of its delicate sensuality. The language of our author, like patent blacking, "would not soil the whitest linen," and yet the composition itself, would suffice, if well laid on, to Ethiopize the snowiest conscience that ever sat like a swan upon that mirror of heaven, a Christian maiden's imagination. We are not sure we speak quite strong enough, when we say, that we would much rather listen to the coarsest scene of Goldsmith's *Vicar,* read aloud by a sister or daughter, than to hear from such lips, the perfectly chaste language of a scene in *The Scarlet Letter,* in which a married wife and her reverend paramour, with their unfortunate offspring, are introduced as the actors, and in which the whole tendency of the conversation is to suggest a sympathy for their sin, and an anxiety that they may be able to accomplish a successful escape beyond the seas, to some country where their shameful commerce may be perpetuated. Now, in Goldsmith's story there are very coarse words, but we do not remember anything that saps the foundations of the moral sense, or that goes to create unavoidable sympathy with unrepenting sorrow, and deliberate, premeditated sin. *The Vicar of Wakefield* is sometimes coarsely virtuous, but *The Scarlet Letter* is delicately immoral.

—Arthur Cleveland Coxe, "The Writings of Hawthorne," *Church Review and Ecclesiastical Register* 3, No. 3 (January 1851): 506–7

[Henry James (1843–1916), perhaps the most significant American novelist of his time, was also an occasional critic. He was the author of many book reviews and critical essays, which were assembled in such volumes as *French Poets and Novelists* (1878), *Views and Reviews* (1908), *Notes on Novelists* (1914), and others. His book-length study of Hawthorne was written for the prestigious English Men of Letters series published by Macmillan. In this extract James begins by supplying a vivid recollection of the novel's appearance (he was seven years old at the time), then claiming that Hester Prynne is not the center of the novel but rather the two leading male characters, Dimmesdale and Chillingworth.]

If Hawthorne was in a sombre mood, and if his future was painfully vague, *The Scarlet Letter* contains little enough of gaiety or of hopefulness. It is densely dark, with a single spot of vivid colour in it; and it will probably long remain the most consistently gloomy of English novels of the first order. But I just now called it the author's masterpiece, and I imagine it will continue to be, for other generations than ours, his most substantial title to fame. The subject had probably lain a long time in his mind, as his subjects were apt to do; so that he appears completely to possess it, to know it and feel it. It is simpler and more complete than his other novels; it achieves more perfectly what it attempts, and it has about it that charm, very hard to express, which we find in an artist's work the first time he has touched his highest mark—a sort of straightness and naturalness of execution, an unconsciousness of his public, and freshness of interest in his theme. It was a great success, and he immediately found himself famous. The writer of these lines, who was a child at the time, remembers dimly the sensation the book produced, and the little shudder with which people alluded to it, as if a peculiar horror were mixed with its attractions. He was too young to read it himself; but its title, upon which he fixed his eyes as the book lay upon the table, had a mysterious charm. He had a vague belief, indeed, that the "letter" in question was one of the documents that come by the post, and it was a source of perpetual wonderment to him that it should be of such an unaccustomed hue. Of course it was difficult to explain to a child the significance of poor Hester Prynne's blood-coloured A. But the mystery was at last partly dispelled by his being taken to see a collection of pictures (the annual exhibition of the National Academy), where he encountered a representation of a pale, handsome woman, in a quaint black dress and a white coif, holding between her knees an elfish-looking little girl, fantastically dressed, and crowned with flowers. Embroidered on the woman's breast was a great crimson A, over which the child's fingers, as she glanced strangely out of the picture, were maliciously playing. I was told that this was Hester Prynne and little Pearl, and that when I grew older I might read their interesting history. But the picture remained vividly imprinted on my mind; I had been vaguely frightened and made uneasy by it; and when, years afterwards, I first read the novel, I seemed to myself to have read it before, and to be familiar with its two strange heroines. I mention this incident simply as an indication of the degree to which the success of *The Scarlet Letter* had made the book what is called an actuality. Hawthorne himself was very modest about it; he wrote to his publisher, when there was a question of his undertaking another novel, that what had given the history of Hester Prynne its "vogue" was simply the introductory chapter. In fact, the publication of *The Scarlet Letter* was in the United States a literary event of the first importance. The book was the finest piece of imaginative writing yet put forth in the country. There was a consciousness of this in the welcome that was given it—a satisfaction in the idea of America having produced a novel that belonged to literature, and to the forefront of it. Something might at last be sent to Europe as exquisite in quality as anything that had been received, and the best of it was that the thing was absolutely American; it belonged to the soil, to the air; it came out of the very heart of New England.

It is beautiful, admirable, extraordinary; it has in the highest degree that merit which I have spoken of as the mark of Hawthorne's best things—an indefinable purity and lightness of conception, a quality which in a work of art affects one in the same way as the absence of grossness does in a human being.

His fancy, as I just now said, had evidently brooded over the subject for a long time; the situation to be represented had disclosed itself to him in all its phases. When I say in all its phases, the sentence demands modification; for it is to be remembered that if Hawthorne laid his hand upon the well-worn theme, upon the familiar combination of the wife, the lover, and the husband, it was, after all, but to one period of the history of these three persons that he attached himself. The situation is the situation after the woman's fault has been committed, and the current of expiation and repentance has set in. In spite of the relation between Hester Prynne and Arthur Dimmesdale, no story of love was surely ever less of a "love-story." To Hawthorne's imagination the fact that these two persons had loved each other too well was of an interest comparatively vulgar; what appealed to him was the idea of their moral situation in the long years that were to follow. The story, indeed, is in a secondary degree that of Hester Prynne; she becomes, really, after the first scene, an accessory figure; it is not upon her the *dénoûment* depends. It is upon her guilty lover that the author projects most frequently the cold, thin rays of his fitfully-moving lantern, which makes here and there a little luminous circle, on the edge of which hovers the livid and sinister figure of the injured and retributive husband. The story goes on, for the most part, between the lover and the husband—the tormented young Puritan minister, who carries the secret of his own lapse from pastoral purity locked up beneath an exterior that commends itself to the reverence of his flock, while he sees the softer partner of his guilt standing in the full glare of exposure and humbling herself to the misery of atonement—between this more wretched and pitiable culprit, to whom dishonour would come as a comfort and the pillory as a relief, and the older, keener, wiser man, who, to obtain satisfaction for the wrong he has suffered, devises the infernally ingenious plan of conjoining himself with his wronger, living with him, living upon him; and while he pretends to minister to his hidden ailment and to sympathise with his pain, revels in his unsuspected knowledge of these things, and stimulates them by malignant arts. The attitude of Roger Chillingworth, and the means he takes to compensate himself—these are the highly original elements in the situation that Hawthorne so ingeniously treats.

None of his works are so impregnated with that after-sense of the old Puritan consciousness of life to which allusion has so often been made. If, as M. Montégut says, the qualities of his ancestors *filtered* down through generations into his composition, *The Scarlet Letter* was, as it were, the vessel that gathered up the last of the precious drops. And I say this not because the story happens to be of so-called historical cast, to be told of the early days of Massachusetts, and of people in steeple-crowned hats and sad-coloured garments. The historical colouring is rather weak than otherwise; there is little elaboration of detail, of the modern realism of research; and the author has made no great point of causing his figures to speak the English of their period. Nevertheless, the book is full of the moral presence of the race that invented Hester's penance— diluted and complicated with other things, but still perfectly recognisable. Puritanism, in a word, is there, not only objectively, as Hawthorne tried to place it there, but subjectively as well. Not, I mean, in his judgment of his characters in any harshness of prejudice, or in the obtrusion of a moral lesson; but in the very quality of his own vision, in the tone of the picture, in a certain coldness and exclusiveness of treatment.
—Henry James, *Hawthorne* (London: Macmillan, 1879), pp. 109–14

GEORGE E. WOODBERRY ON HAWTHORNE'S LITERARY DEVELOPMENT

[George E. Woodberry (1855–1930) was an American critic, poet, and biographer. He was a pioneer in the study of comparative literature and taught that discipline at Columbia University. In addition to his biography of Hawthorne, he wrote biographies of Ralph Waldo Emerson (1907) and Edgar Allan Poe (1909), as well as the volume on Poe for the English Men of Letters series (1885). In this extract, Woodberry finds that the basic themes of *The Scarlet Letter* had been present in a nebulous form in many earlier works. This is a good example of the holistic approach to literature, in which the entirety of an author's work is examined for the dominant themes or motifs running through it.]

The Scarlet Letter is a great and unique romance, standing apart by itself in fiction; there is nothing else quite like it. Of all Hawthorne's works it is most identified with his genius in popular regard, and it has the peculiar power that is apt to invest the first work of an author in which his originality finds complete artistic expression. It is seldom that one can observe so plainly the different elements that are primary in a writer's endowment coalesce in the fully developed work of genius; yet in this romance there is nothing either in method or perception which is not to be found in the earlier tales; what distinguishes it is the union of art and intuition as they had grown up in Hawthorne's practice and had developed a power to penetrate more deeply into life. Obviously at the start there is the physical object in which his imagination habitually found its spring, the fantastically embroidered scarlet letter on a woman's bosom which he had seen in the Puritan group described in "Endicott and the Red Cross." It had been in his mind for years, and his thoughts had centered on it and wandered out from it, tracking its mystery. It has in itself that decorative quality, which he sought in the physical object,—the brilliant and rich effect, startling to the eye and yet more to the imagination as it blazes forth with a secret symbolism and almost intelligence of its own. It multiplies itself, as the tale unfolds, with greater intensity and mysterious significance and dread suggestion, as if in mirrors set round about it,—in the slowly disclosed and fearful stigma on the minister's hidden heart over which he ever holds his hand, where it has become flesh of his flesh; in the growing elf-like figure of the child, who, with her eyes always fastened on the open shame of the letter on her mother's bosom or the hidden secret of the hand on her father's breast, has become herself the symbol, half revealed and half concealed, is dressed in it, as every reader remembers, and fantastically embodies it as if the thing had taken life in her; and, as if this were not enough, the scarlet letter, at a climax of the dark story, lightens forth over the whole heavens as a symbol of what cannot be hid even in the intensest blackness of night. The continual presence of the letter seems to have burnt into Hawthorne's own mind, till at the end of the narrative he says he would gladly erase its deep print from the brain where long meditation had fixed it. In no other work is the physical symbol so absorbingly present, so reduplicated, so much alive in itself. It is the brand of sin on life. Its concrete vividness leads the author also by a natural compulsion as well as an artistic instinct to display his story in that succession of high-wrought scenes, tableaux, in fact, which was his characteristic method of narrative, picturesque, pictorial, almost to be described as theatrical in spectacle. The background, also, as in the early tales, is of the slightest, no more than will suffice for the acting of the drama as a stage setting sympathetic with the central scene,— a town, with a prison, a meeting-house, a pillory, a governor's house, other habitations on a street, a lonely cottage by the shore, the forest round about all; and for occasion and accessories, only a woman's sentence, the incidental death of Winthrop unmarked in itself, a buccaneering ship in the harbor, Indians, Spanish sailors, rough matrons, clergy; this will serve, for such was Hawthorne's fine economy, knowing that this story was one in which every materialistic element must be used at its lowest tone. Though the scene lay in this world, it was but transitory scaffolding; the drama was one of the eternal life.

The characteristic markings of Hawthorne's genius are also to be found in other points. He does not present the scene of life, the crowd of the world with its rich and varied fullness of interest, complexity of condition and movement, and its interwoven texture of character, event, and fate, such as the great novelists use; he has only a few individual figures, and these are simplified by being exhibited, not in their complete lives, but only in that single aspect of their experience which was absorbing to themselves and constituted the life they lived in the soul itself. There are three characters, Hester, the minister, and the physician; and a fourth, the child, who fulfills the function of the chorus in the old drama, in part a living comment, in part a spectator and medium of sympathy with the main actors. In all four of these that trait of profound isolation in life, so often used before in the earlier tales, is strongly brought out; about each is struck a circle which separates not only one from another, but from all the world, and in the midst of it, as in a separate orb, each lives an unshared life. It is inherent, too, in such a situation that the mystery that had fascinated Hawthorne in so many forms, the secrecy of men's bosoms, should be a main theme in the treatment. He has also had recourse to that method of violent contrast which has been previously illustrated; on the one hand the publicity of detected wrongdoing, on the other the hidden and unsuspected fact; here the open shame and there the secret sin, whose sameness in a double life is expressed by the identity of the embroidered letter and the flesh-wrought stigma. But it is superfluous to illustrate further the genesis of this romance out of Hawthorne's art and matter in his earlier work, showing how naturally it rose by a concentration of his powers on a single theme that afforded them scope, intensity, and harmony at once. The new thing here is the power of his genius to penetrate, as was said above, deep into life.

—George E. Woodberry, *Nathaniel Hawthorne* (New York: Houghton Mifflin, 1902), pp. 189–93

MARK VAN DOREN ON HESTER PRYNNE IN CONFLICT WITH HER SOCIETY

[Mark Van Doren (1894–1972), the younger brother of Carl Van Doren, was an American critic, poet, and novelist. His *Collected Poems* (1939) won a Pulitzer Prize. Among his critical works are *Henry David Thoreau* (1916) and *The Poetry of John Dryden* (1931). In this extract, Van Doren admires the characterization of Hester Prynne and—in what might be regarded as a proto-feminist analysis—shows how Hester triumphs over her repressive society by her inner strength.]

Above all it is Hester Prynne, whose passion and beauty dominate every other person, and color each event. Hawthorne has conceived her as he has conceived his scene, in the full strength of his feeling for ancient New England. He is the Homer of that New England, as Hester is its most heroic creature. Tall, with dark and abundant hair and deep black eyes, a rich complexion that makes modern women (says Hawthorne) pale and thin by comparison, and a dignity that throws into low relief the "delicate, evanescent, and indescribable grace" by which gentility in girls has since come to be known, from the very first—and we believe it—she is said to cast a spell over those who behold her; and this is not merely because of the scarlet letter, "so fantastically embroidered and illuminated," upon the bosom of her always magnificent dress. It is because of herself, into whom Hawthorne has known how to put a unique importance. Nor is this a remote, a merely stately importance. We are close to her all of the time, and completely convinced of her flesh and blood, of her heart and mind. She is a passionate woman whom Hawthorne does not need to call passionate, for he has the evidence: her state of excitement, bordering on frenzy, in the prison after her first exposure to the crowd—her "moral agony," reflected in the convulsions that have seized the child; her pride, her daring, in after days when she makes more show than she needs to make of the letter on her bosom, the symbol she insists upon adorning with such "wild and picturesque peculiarity"; her alternations of despair and defiance; her continuing love, so unconfessed that we can only assume it to be there, for the man whose weakness seems so little to deserve it; her power of speech, so economical and so tender, when at last she is with this man; her sudden revelation that through years of loneliness she has not consented to let her soul be killed.

"I pity thee," says Chillingworth near the close, "for the good that has been wasted in thy nature." These are terrible words, for they express a fear we have had, the fear that this magnificent woman has lived for nothing; for a few days of love, and then for dreary years of less indeed than nothing. Hawthorne has known how to fasten this fear upon us—it could exist in us only if we loved her too—but he also has known how to make Chillingworth's words untrue. The life of Hester increases, not diminishes, in the bleak world whose best citizen she is. Nor is this done by Hawthorne at the expense of that world. He deplores the "dismal severity" of its moral code, and for all we know he is presenting Hester as the blackest sacrifice it ever offered on its altar. But he is not doctrinaire against the code.

His Puritan world is in its own way beautiful. It fully exists, as Hester fully exists. If their existences conflict, then that is the tragedy to be understood. Hester, whose solitary thought takes her far beyond the confines of the code, is nevertheless respectful of the strength in it that could kill her were she not even stronger. She is not the subject of a sermon; she is the heroine of a tragedy, and she understands the tragedy. She understands it because Hawthorne does; because at the same time that he recoils from the Puritan view of sin he honors its capacity to be a view at all. Sin for him, for Hester, and for the people who punish her is equally a solemn fact, a problem for which there is no solution in life. There was no other solution for his story, given Hester's strength, Dimmesdale's weakness, and Chillingworth's perversion, than the one he found. Rather, as we read, it finds itself. And if the conclusion is not depressing, the reason is that nothing before it has been meaningless. This world has not been really bleak. It has been as beautiful as it was terrible; Hester's life has not been hollow, nor has her great nature been wasted.

—Mark Van Doren, *Nathaniel Hawthorne* (New York: William Sloane Associates, 1949), pp. 150–53

LESLIE A. FIEDLER ON "GOTHIC" ELEMENTS IN *THE SCARLET LETTER*

[Leslie A. Fiedler (b. 1917), the Samuel L. Clemens Professor of Literature at the State University of New York at Buffalo, is a leading American literary critic and advocate of the literary and cultural significance of popular literature. Among his many books are *Waiting for the End* (1964), *The Return of the Vanishing American* (1968), *Collected Essays* (1971), and *What Was Literature? Class Culture and Mass Society* (1982). In this extract, from his pioneering study *Love and Death in the American Novel* (1960), Fiedler studies the relation of *The Scarlet Letter* to the supernatural or "Gothic" novels of the late eighteenth and early nine-

teenth centuries, especially the British writer Ann
Radcliffe (1764–1823) and the American novelist
Charles Brockden Brown (1771–1810).]

The Scarlet Letter is finally not essentially a love story at all; and
though it is possible to gain some insights into its theme and
tone by considering it an American, which is to say, a dena-
tured and defleshed, *Nouvelle Héloïse,* ⟨a novel by Jean-
Jacques Rousseau⟩ it is more valuable to approach it as an
American, which is to say, a less violent and hopeless, version
of *The Monk.* Like ⟨Matthew Gregory⟩ Lewis' horror novel,
Hawthorne's little book deals with a man of God led by the
desire for a woman to betray his religious commitment, and
finally almost (Hawthorne repents at the last moment, as Lewis
does not) to sell his soul to the Devil. Certainly, it makes more
sense to compare the figure of Hester with that of the active
Matilda, and Dimmesdale with the passive Ambrosio, who is
seduced by her, than to try to find analogues for the American
pair in Goethe's Gretchen and Faust. If Hawthorne's novella is,
indeed, as has often been suggested, an American *Faust,* it is a
Faust without a traduced maiden. Much less sentimental and
Richardsonian than Goethe, Hawthorne is not concerned with
the fall of innocence at the seducer's hand or with that seducer's salvation by the prayers of his victim.

The Faustianism of Hawthorne is the melodramatic
Faustianism of the gothic romancers: of Lewis, whom he read
avidly, and of ⟨Charles Robert⟩ Maturin, from whose *Melmoth
the Wanderer* he borrowed the name of a minor character in
Fanshawe. Not only Lewis and Maturin, but Mrs. Radcliffe and
Brockden Brown were favorite authors of the young
Hawthorne; and from them he learned how to cast on events
the lurid light, the air of equivocal terror which gives its "hell-
fired" atmosphere. The very color scheme of the book, the
black-and-whiteness of its world illuminated only by the baleful
glow of the scarlet letter, come from the traditional gothic
palette; but in Hawthorne's imagination, those colors are
endowed with a moral significance. Black and white are not
only the natural colors of the wintry forest settlement in which
the events unfold, but stand, too, for that settlement's rigidly
distinguished versions of virtue and vice; while red is the color
of sexuality itself, the fear of which haunts the Puritan world

like a bloody specter. The book opens with a description of "the black flower of civilized society, a prison" and closes on a gravestone, a "simple slab of slate," whose escutcheon is "sombre . . . and relieved only by one ever-glowing point of light gloomier than a shadow:—ON A FIELD SABLE, THE LETTER A, GULES."

It is the scarlet letter itself which is finally the chief gothic property of Hawthorne's tale, more significant than the portents and signs, the meteors in the midnight sky, or even "the noise of witches; whose voices, at that period, were often heard . . . as they rode with Satan through the air. . . ." Into that letter are compressed the meanings of all the demonic fires, scarlet blossoms, and red jewels which symbolize passion and danger in his earlier tales. It glows with a heat genital and Satanic at once—burning his fingers even centuries later, Hawthorne tells us in his introduction, like "red-hot iron"; and its "lurid gleam," the text declares, is derived "from the flames of the infernal pit." Its "bale-fire," at any rate, lights up the book with a flickering glare representing at once Hester's awareness of guilt and Hawthorne's: his doubts over his plunge into the unconscious, and hers over her fall through passion into the lawless world of Nature.

The wearer of such a sign is transformed into a gothic villainess-heroine: a taboo figure, utterly alienated from the world of the unfallen, yet capable of bestowing on that world, in its moments of pain and death, a signal kind of relief. Worn openly, the genital brand, "red-hot with internal fire," becomes a sacred charm, like the cross on a nun's bosom; grants powers of healing, immunity to Indians, a strange and terrible insight into the sinfulness of others. What Hester inwardly perceives the book makes explicit: that the scarlet letter belongs not to her alone but to the whole community which has sought to exclude her. It is repeated everywhere: in the child she bears, who is the scarlet letter made flesh; in the heavens of secret midnight; on the tombstone which takes up her monitory role after she is dead; and especially in the secret sign on the breast of the minister, whom the community considers its special saint. In his dumb flesh is confessed what his articulate mouth cannot avow, not his transgression alone but that of all men who have cast the first stone. At the heart of the American past, in the parchment scroll which is our history, Hawthorne has discovered not an original innocence but a primal guilt— and he seeks to evoke that past not in nostalgia but terror.

—Leslie A. Fiedler, "*The Scarlet Letter:* Woman as Faust," *Love and Death in the American Novel* (New York: Criterion Books, 1960), pp. 508–10

DANIEL HOFFMAN ON THE ALLEGORICAL FUNCTION OF PEARL

[Daniel Hoffman (b. 1923), a professor of English and poet-in-residence at the University of Pennsylvania, is a leading American poet and critic. He has written *The Poetry of Stephen Crane* (1957) and *Poe Poe Poe Poe Poe Poe Poe* (1972), and is the editor of *The Harvard Guide to Contemporary American Writing* (1979). In this extract, Hoffman focuses on Hester's daughter, Pearl, whom he sees as a symbol for the pagan sexuality exhibited by Hester.]

Many modern readers find Hester's elf-child intolerably arch, with her pranks and preternatural knowledge. She is indeed a remarkable infant, distinguished as much for her fidelity to the actual psychology of a three-year-old child as for the allegorism with which Hawthorne manipulates her strange behavior. Her fixation upon the 'A' might seem completely arbitrary, yet children of that age do indeed become attached to familiar objects in just such a fashion. Pearl was closely modelled on Hawthorne's own little daughter Una. And if Una was named for Spenser's allegorical heroine, Pearl, as Mr. Male remarks, takes her name from the passage in Matthew which signifies truth and grace. When Hester strips herself of the scarlet letter she regains her pagan sexuality in the heathen world of Nature, beyond human law and divine truth. She has also taken off a token familiar to Pearl since earliest infancy. Both literally and figuratively, her child must resent her changed appearance until the familiar badge of discipline is resumed.

At one point Pearl amuses herself by mimicking her mother. She has been gazing into a pool in the woods, 'seeking a passage for herself into its [reflected] sphere of impalpable earth and unattainable sky.' Her attempt to merge herself into the elements is unavailing, and she turns to other tricks. She makes herself a mantle of seaweed, and, 'As the last touch to her mermaid's garb, Pearl took some eel-grass, and imitated, as best she could, on her own bosom . . . the letter A,—but freshly green instead of scarlet!' When Hester beholds her handiwork she says, 'My little Pearl, the green letter, on thy childish bosom, has no purport. But dost thou know, my child, what this letter means which thy mother is doomed to wear?' Pearl, with her preternatural intuition, answers 'Truly do I! It is for the same reason that the minister keeps his hand over his heart!' But Hester cannot bear to tell her what she seems already to know, and breaks off, saying, 'I wear it for the sake of its gold thread.'

This scene perhaps seems a digression which fails to advance our understanding of either Hester or Pearl. But in fact it comprises a metaphoric recapitulation and explanation of the nature of Hester's offense. Pearl's allegorical function brings into *The Scarlet Letter* the pagan values which Hawthorne had synthesized in "The Maypole at Merry Mount." But in *The Scarlet Letter* the amoral freedom of the green natural world is viewed with yet greater reservations than was true of his story, written fifteen years earlier. We have already noticed that the forest is described, in Hester's rendezvous with Dimmesdale, as 'wild, heathen Nature.' The child will not let her mother cast the scarlet letter aside because Pearl herself is emblem of a passion which partook of that same heathen, natural wildness. 'What we did had a consecration of its own,' Hester assures Arthur, but that consecration was not a Christian or a moral sanctity. It was an acknowledgment of the life force itself. Consequently Pearl is endowed with the morally undirected energies of life. 'The spell of life went forth from her ever creative spirit, and communicated itself to a thousand objects, as a torch kindles a flame wherever it may be applied.' This spell is the power of fecundity, and its derivative power, that of imagination. 'The unlikeliest materials—a stick, a bunch of rags, a flower—were the puppets of Pearl's witchcraft . . .' These she brings to life, and she feels in herself kinship with life in every form. Although the forest is a place of dread and evil, the haunt of witches and of heathen Indian sorcerers, Pearl is at home among its creatures. It 'became the playmate of the lonely infant' and 'put on the kindest of moods to welcome her.' Squirrels fling their treasured nuts to Pearl, while even wolves and foxes take caresses from her hand. 'The mother-forest, and those wild things which it nourished, all recognized a kindred wildness in the human child.'

It was in this mother-forest that Hester had had her tryst with Dimmesdale, beyond human law and divine truth. Hester herself sees that 'The child could not be made amenable to rules. In giving her existence, a great law had been broken; and the result was a being whose elements were perhaps beautiful and brilliant, but all in disorder.'

—Daniel Hoffman, "Hester's Double Providence: The Scarlet Letter and the Green," *Form and Fable in American Fiction* (New York: Oxford University Press, 1961), pp. 178–80

A. N. KAUL ON HAWTHORNE AS CRITIC OF RELIGION

[A. N. Kaul, formerly a professor of English at Yale University, is the author of *The Action of English Comedy* (1970) and editor of *Hawthorne: A Collection of Critical Essays* (1966). In this extract, Kaul studies Hawthorne's portrayal of the social and religious environment of Puritan New England from the position of both an outspoken critic and a sympathetic "insider."]

In reading *The Scarlet Letter* it is necessary to remember that this is a book about and not of seventeenth-century New England. There is a danger, that is to say, of confusing the subject of the novel with the novelist's attitude, especially because the latter involves an irony which often assumes the innocent guise of approval. In many ways Hawthorne was undoubtedly the heir of the Puritan tradition, but he was also one of its severest critics. His criticism, more searching and sustained than that of Fenimore Cooper before him, has at times the damaging effectiveness, without the invective, of the Smart Set's guerilla attacks in the twentieth century. For instance, his comment on the portraits in Governor Bellingham's house—"as if they were the ghosts, rather than the pictures, of departed worthies, and were gazing with harsh and intolerant criticism at the pursuits and enjoyments of living men"—recalls Mencken's quick-fire definition of Puritanism as "the haunting fear that someone, somewhere may be happy." ⟨. . .⟩

Hawthorne himself was several thankful generations away from the Pilgrim Fathers. Actually he lived in the same generation with Emerson. But to state in this manner the distance that separates him from the subject of his novel can be misleading. Unlike Emerson, he was not cut off from the Puritans by the impassable peak of a novel and exciting theory of the cosmos. Nor did he view them as Cooper did—across the limitless spaces of the Hudson River. His attitude toward his subject suggests a complex relation rather than an intractable and artistically sterile distance. On account of his personal temperament, his artistic sensibility, and his family history, he could approach the seventeenth century as an insider, retaining at the same time the outsider's ability and freedom to judge and evaluate. Like so many great works of literature—Arthur Koestler's *Darkness at Noon* is a notable modern example— *The Scarlet Letter* is a searching criticism of the world with which it deals precisely because it takes its stand firmly within that world.

⟨. . .⟩ Of course, the effectiveness of Hawthorne's novel arises not from any general doctrine but from the rich particularity with which he explores a definite historical phase of society as well as the fate of individuals in it. It is characteristic of his temper and times again, however, that he should set out on his evaluation of the Puritan settlement by conceding its importance as a utopian experiment. "The founders of a new colony," we read on the first page of the novel, "whatever utopia of human virtue and happiness they might originally project, have invariably recognized it among their earliest practical necessities to allot a portion of the virgin soil as a cemetery, and another portion as the site of a prison."

—A. N. Kaul, "Nathaniel Hawthorne: Heir and Critic of the Puritan Tradition," *The American Vision: Actual and Ideal Society in Nineteenth-Century Fiction* (New Haven: Yale University Press, 1963), pp. 173–76

HYATT H. WAGGONER ON HESTER PRYNNE AS TRAGIC HEROINE

[Hyatt H. Waggoner (1913–1988) was for many years a professor of American civilization at Brown University and one of the leading scholars of American literature. He is the author of an important volume, *Hawthorne: A Critical Study* (1955), as well as such other books as *Emerson as Poet* (1974) and *American Visionary Poetry* (1982). In this extract, taken from a collection of his essays on Hawthorne, Waggoner studies the role of Hester as a tragic heroine in embodying the eternal conflict of nature and society.]

For Hawthorne, the focal point of his story, I suspect, was the fate of a young woman married to an old man. Scholars who have uncovered the "sources" of *The Scarlet Letter* in New England's history have found the passages in Hawthorne's favorite reading that probably suggested to him the penalty of having to wear the scarlet letter, the name "Hester" for his heroine, and much more. But the history of Mary Latham, married to an old and (presumably) impotent man, a girl who committed adultery with "divers young men," was probably the story that ignited his imagination. It was very likely her story that prompted his notebook entry in 1844 or 1845, "The life of a woman, who, by the old colony law, was condemned always to wear the letter A, sewed on her garment, in token of her having committed adultery." What was such a person to do, in a society that demanded and enforced repression of sexual impulses except as they could be satisfied in marriage? What "happy" outcome for her *could* there be?

When he finally came to write his novel Hawthorne did everything he could do without committing himself to open approval of her defiance of Puritan morality to make us sympathize with Hester, who knowingly defied the Puritan code and who dreamed of a day in the future, beyond her time, when women would be considered as people, not property. In the beginning of his tale, Hawthorne gave Hester great beauty and vitality, and a halo; at the end, he knew he had made her a tragic heroine who had managed, by the strength of her courage and integrity, to find meaning and purpose in life despite her frustration.

He could think of no "happy ending" for her, no escape that could be made plausible. He did not think her "innocent," but he did consider her a victim. Her tale, when his wife read it to him, moved him more than any of his later novels would have the power to do. Could any escape from frustration be imagined? He thought perhaps it could—at least for those more fortunately placed than Hester and Dimmesdale—and quickly undertook to write a happier work, *The House of the Seven Gables,* which he would later describe as more "representative" of him. In a sense he would be right, but only half: the self it represented was more the ideal self-image, the man he wished to be, than the total man. It better suggested what he believed but less powerfully embodied what he felt.

Hawthorne's sensibility and outlook more closely and clearly foreshadow Robert Penn Warren's than do those of any other nineteenth-century American writer of fiction. His tensions between desire and belief, feeling and thought, have been Warren's. In theme, image, and situation, Hawthorne's fiction, especially his short tales, anticipates the fiction of Warren. The "Hawthorne tradition" in American fiction runs through Melville to James (despite James's effort to break free from it) to Faulkner to Warren. What this whole tradition leaves unclear is whether there is any—any conceivable, any possible— escape from the consequences of "human frailty," any emotion possible to conceive besides "sorrow."

For Hawthorne, when he wrote *The Scarlet Letter,* the cemetery and the prison of the opening chapter were undeniably evident in life. The rose, which he hoped might serve to "symbolize some sweet ["fulfilling"? "self-realizing"?] moral [fulfilling but not condemned, not "guilt-producing"?] blossom [flowers, like Hester, are beautiful and, also like her, feel no guilt], that may be found along the track, or relieve the darkening close of a tale of human frailty and sorrow"—for Hawthorne, the rose could only be postulated and hoped for. In this novel at least, Hawthorne's most deeply felt, it could not be found.

Can it be found—and found to be authentic, not just professed or wished for—granted that as we look back through history it seems mostly not to have been found, except perhaps by the mystics and the saints? Can guilty, suffering, and dying man find fulfillment of his conflicting desires to satisfy himself and at the same time love and be loved by others? Can he find a way to be himself and yet live in community with others, to be true at once to "nature" and to "society"?

If he can, he must do so without denying the tragic truths Hawthorne's novel so beautifully embodies. *The Scarlet Letter* is Hawthorne's finest expression of his feeling of "the way life is." Emerson's effort to tell us how it *might* be for the enlightened was not Hawthorne's subject here. As he wrote to his publisher about what he was creating, "*The Scarlet Letter* is positively a hell-fired story, into which I find it almost impossible to throw any cheering light." To most of us today, the story is likely to seem not so much "hell-fired" as true to ordinary experience as most people suffer it most of the time.

> —Hyatt H. Waggoner, "Dark Light on the Letter" (1968), *The Presence of Hawthorne* (Baton Rouge: Louisiana State University Press, 1979), pp. 73–75

MICHAEL DAVITT BELL ON HESTER PRYNNE AS REBEL

[Michael Davitt Bell (b. 1941) is J. Lelend Miller Professor of American History, Literature, and Eloquence at Williams College (Williamstown, MA). He is the author of *The Development of American Romance* (1980), *The Sentiment of Reality: Truth of Feeling in the European Novel* (1983), and *The Problem of American Realism* (1993). In this essay, Bell investigates Hawthorne's attitude toward Hester Prynne by noting his many hostile remarks on "rebellious" women. According to Bell, Hawthorne intends the reader to contrast Hester with the seventeenth-century religious rebel Ann Hutchinson, the subject of Hawthorne's earlier sketch, "Mrs. Hutchinson" (1830).]

It is of crucial importance to note that what Hawthorne approves in his heroine is not her rebelliousness, however splendid that quality may sometimes seem, but rather her ability to *overcome* that rebelliousness and assume the feminine qualities of domesticity. For the great difference between Hester and Hawthorne's earlier female outcasts is that Hester returns to her obligations and subordinate position. Unlike Catharine in "The Gentle Boy," Hester Prynne does not abandon her child. Hawthorne surely agrees with Dimmesdale's argument, at Bellingham's mansion, that there is "a quality of awful sacredness in the relation between this mother and this child." Hawthorne believes with Dimmesdale that the child was meant, "above all things else, to keep the mother's soul alive, and to preserve her from blacker depths of sin into which Satan might else have sought to plunge her!"

What these "blacker depths" are is made clear in Chapter XIII, entitled "Another View of Hester." Hester, we learn, is on the verge of falling into feminism, into an open defiance of tradition and authority. "The world's law," we are told, "was no law for her mind." Hester envisions a change in the role of women, a change Hawthorne regards with horror. For with this change, Hawthorne insists, "the ethereal essence, wherein [woman] was her truest life, will be found to have evaporated." Hester risks being transformed permanently into a Catharine or an Anne Hutchinson. "She might," Hawthorne writes, "have come down to us in history, hand in hand with Ann Hutchinson, as the foundress of a religious sect. She might, in one of her phrases, have been a prophetess. She might, and not improbably would, have suffered death from the stern tribunals of the period, for attempting to undermine the foundations of the Puritan establishment." All this might have happened, we are told, "had little Pearl never come to her from the spiritual world." Hester is saved by Pearl. "Providence," Hawthorne continues, "in the person of this little girl, had assigned to Hester's charge the germ and blossom of womanhood, to be cherished and developed amid a host of difficulties." Like Catharine in "The Gentle Boy," Hester has a choice between following the whims of her fancy or following her duties as a mother. But unlike Catharine she chooses the latter. No more than "Mrs. Hutchinson" does *The Scarlet Letter* glorify female self-assertion. To the extent that Hester forges something positive out of the aftermath of her sin, her success represents a triumph not of rebellion but of subordination.

—Michael Davitt Bell, "Another View of Hester," *Hawthorne and the Historical Romance of New England* (Princeton: Princeton University Press, 1971), pp. 179–80

ROBERT H. FOSSUM ON DIMMESDALE AS A CHRIST FIGURE

[Robert H. Fossum is a literary scholar and author of *William Styron: A Critical Study* (1968) and *Hawthorne's Inviolable Circle: The Problem of Time* (1972), from which the following extract is taken. Here Fossum studies the character of Dimmesdale, finding provocative parallels with the crucifixion and death of Jesus Christ.]

For Dimmesdale, Election Day marks his birth as a new man. Ironically, it is also the day in which he is elected to pass out of time into eternity. Hester unsuspectingly says as much in explaining the significance of the occasion to Pearl: " 'For today, a new man is beginning to rule over them; and so—as has been the custom of mankind ever since a nation was first gathered—they make merry and rejoice; as if a good and golden year were at length to pass over the poor old world.' " Ascending the platform with Hester and Pearl, Dimmesdale elects to expose his past and—as Chillingworth's exclamation, " 'Thou hast escaped me!' ", suggests—to exorcise its power over him. Now in one sense his action doesn't save him at all. Still believing primarily in a God of vengeance rather than a God of mercy, doubtful that grace and forgiveness follow from a true act of contrition, Dimmesdale remains a victim of the old dispensation; his confession is merely the "last expression of the despondency of a broken spirit." Yet in another sense it does. His acknowledgment of Hester, and, more particularly, of Pearl as the "tie that united them," restores the circle, temporal and domestic, which he has broken. Releasing him from his bondage to the past, it unites him with the part of himself which has an earthly future. It humanizes that future, too, for the "great scene of grief, in which the wild infant bore a part, had developed all her sympathies; and as her tears fell upon her father's cheek, they were the pledge that she would grow up amid human joy and sorrow, nor forever do battle with the world, but be a woman in it."

The question of Dimmesdale's spiritual future is another matter, one which Hawthorne does not presume to answer. He hints at an answer, however, by drawing parallels between the minister and Christ, between Dimmesdale's last agonies and the crucifixion, between Dimmesdale's confession and the Christian doctrine that to save one's life one must lose it. The parallels also recall the idea, introduced at the beginning of the book, that everything pertaining to sin is timeless; they repeat the suggestion, implicit throughout, that each man recreates in his own life span the spiritual history of the race from Adam's sin to its expiation by Christ; they even seem to imply that every man is a potential Christ who to achieve transformation must submit to a type of crucifixion.

The first parallel occurs in Dimmesdale's sermon, which has a vatic spirit like that of the Old Testament prophets, "only with this difference, that, whereas the Jewish seers had denounced judgments and ruin on their country, it was his mission to foretell a high and glorious destiny for the newly gathered people of the Lord"—people composed of a typical American mixture of old and young, Puritans and frontiersmen, Indians and those equally wild barbarians of the "wilderness of ocean," piratical sailors. Dimmesdale, previously locked in the past, now envisions a future in which a new "relation between the Deity and the communities of mankind will be established, with a special reference to the New England which they were here planting in the wilderness." As Christ's death marked the end of an old order and the beginning of a new, so Dimmesdale, near the end of his "transitory stay on earth," prophesies a new era in American history. To his audience, at any rate, the minister is the image of Christ, or at least the image of an "angel [who], in his passage to the skies, had shaken his bright wings over the people for an instant,—at once a shadow and a splendor,—and had shed down a shower of golden truths upon them." Ironic though the parallels may be in light of the minister's subsequent revelation, Dimmesdale is about to elect a kind of cruci-fixion—not only for the sake of his immortal soul but, in a way, for the sins of the Puritan community he stands for: its hypocrisy, its iron attachment to tradition and the letter of the law, its mercilessness. Viewed in this light, his death is a ritual-istic sacrifice of the culture-hero, the Christ-like scapegoat, with the result that the community is freed of at least one spirit of a decadent, demanding past. It is freed of Roger Chillingworth.

The parallels to Christ are established more overtly and the dramatic irony enriched in the procession following the ser-mon. There seems to be a halo about the minister's head; his feet seem hardly to "tread upon the dust of earth"; "feeble and pale he looked amid all his triumph"; and, though he "tottered on his path," he "did not fall." So sublime does he appear, in fact, that the people think it would not have seemed miracu-lous "had he ascended before their eyes, waxing dimmer and brighter, and fading at last into the light of heaven." But where-as the people are unaware of what Dimmesdale is about to do, Hawthorne and his readers are not. From the community's point of view, the procession may recall Christ's triumphal entry into Jerusalem; to us, it suggests the stations of the Cross. Christ knew that His procession led to Calvary; Dimmesdale knows that his journey is toward ignominy on that scaffold where, as ⟨Roy R.⟩ Male puts it, "time and eternity intersect."

The irony of the parallels is revealed to all when Dimmesdale mounts his cross, the place he has privately visited both physi-cally and psychologically so often before. During his sermon he had brought his view of the future before the present; now he unveils the past, telling his listeners that he is not, as they think, so pure and heavenly, but rather (in a phrase confirming his still inverted pride), the " 'one sinner of the world' " with " 'his own red stigma' " on his breast. Even in this instance, however, the parallel—ending with Dimmesdale's final words, " 'His will be done!' "—is only partially ironic. True, by substitut-ing "His" for the more intimate "Thy," Dimmesdale suggests the great distance he still senses between himself and God. Nevertheless, as he confesses, the dying man has a "flush of tri-umph on his face, as one who, in the crisis of acutest pain, had won a victory." In some ways he has been victorious. Dimmesdale's death, like Christ's, has been one of " 'triumphant ignominy,' " a sacrifice without which not only he but, Hawthorne suggests, Pearl and all she stands for would have been forever lost. By freeing himself from the demonic grip of the past, Dimmesdale has presumably ransomed his soul's future and given Pearl a place in time.

—Robert H. Fossum, Hawthorne's Inviolable Circle: The Problem of Time (Deland, FL: Everett/Edwards, 1972), pp. 122–25

ROBERT PENN WARREN ON THE CONFLICT OF NATURE AND SOCIETY

[Robert Penn Warren (1905–1989) was one of the most significant poets, novelists, and critics of the twentieth century. His novel *All the King's Men* (1946) won the Pulitzer Prize. He was one of the founders of the New Criticism, a school of criticism that advocated close study of the text without reference to biographical or other factors outside the work. His textbooks, *Understanding Poetry* (1938) and *Understanding Fiction* (1943), compiled with Cleanth Brooks, were very influential. His best critical essays are included in *Selected Essays* (1958). He also wrote studies of John Greenleaf Whittier (1971) and Theodore Dreiser (1971). In this extract, Warren warns against viewing Hawthorne as entirely on the side of Hester and hostile to the society in which she lives; Warren instead sees the essence of the novel as a conflict between human beings' natural instincts and the moral and social constraints required by society.]

⟨. . .⟩ it may be recalled that, just as *The Scarlet Letter* was often misread as a cautionary tale of sin and conscience, it could also be misread as a tract in which Hester is primarily a martyr for the liberation of women—and of men, too—from a sexually repressive society. Such was the interpretation in a transcendentalist discussion of the novel by a certain George Bailey Loring, a young physician, writing in Theodore Parker's *Massachusetts Quarterly Review*—transcendentalist in so far as the doctrine of "self-reliance" and the validity of "intuition" were taken to imply sexual release from the sanctions of both church and state.

This element of conflict between the individual and society is clearly present in *The Scarlet Letter,* and it is reasonable to suppose that the influence of the Transcendentalists may have sharpened it in Hawthorne's mind. But Hawthorne's concern with the rigors of Puritan society, as with the complex tensions of sexual encounters, long preceded the initial meeting of earnest seekers in George Ripley's study that is usually understood to have officially ushered in the movement.

The meaning of *The Scarlet Letter* is far more tangled and profound than Dr. Loring ever imagined, and bears no simple relation to transcendental reformism. The concern of Hawthorne here, as in his work in general, lies in the tension between the demands of spirit and those of nature. Indeed, the Transcendentalists had insisted upon this issue, but Hawthorne's view, profoundly ironical as it was in seeing the tension between the two realms as the very irremediable essence of life, in its tragedy and glory and even comedy, was far different from anything that ever crossed a transcendental mind.

Even nature, which, in the novel, is thematically set against the sanctions of society, cannot be taken simply. The forest is a haunt of evil as well as of good, and the wishes of the heart may be wicked as well as benign. In the tale "The Holocaust," for example, when all the marks of evil and vanity have been consigned to the flames, the world is not purged; there remains the human heart. In that world of ambiguities, there is, inevitably, a terrible illogic. Good and bad may be intertwined; good may be wasted; accident, not justice, rules. Man is doomed to live in a world where nature is denied and human nature distorted, and—most shatteringly of all—in a world where love and hate may be "the same thing at bottom", and even vice or virtue may represent nothing more than what Chillingworth calls "a typical illusion". But men must live by the logic of their illusions, as best they can—Dimmesdale by his, Hester by hers, and Chillingworth by his. That is their last and darkest "necessity". What compensation is possible in such a world comes from the human capacity for achieving scale and grandeur even in illusion—one might say by insisting on the coherence of the illusion—and from the capacity for giving pity. And here we must remind ourselves that Hawthorne found it "almost impossible to throw a cheering light" on the book.

—Robert Penn Warren, "Hawthorne Revisited: Some Remarks on Hellfiredness," *Sewanee Review* 81, No. 1 (January–March 1973): 110–11

Gloria C. Erlich on Pearl, Dimmesdale, and Chillingworth

[Gloria C. Erlich is a founding member and president of the Princeton Research Forum and author of *The Sexual Education of Edith Wharton* (1992). In this extract, from her earlier book *Family Themes and Hawthorne's Fiction* (1984), Erlich studies the character of Pearl and the complexities of her relationship to her biological father (Dimmesdale) and her socially recognized "father" (Chillingworth). Erlich also finds a parallel between Pearl's paternity and Hawthorne's own loss of his father when he was five years old.]

Pearl's eldritch quality stems directly from the intensity of her search for paternal recognition. Lacking overt clues, she developed uncanny intuitive gifts. She had to search through her mother to discern her father, to sift and study Hester's relationship to men, to become an observer of the slightest gestures and behaviors of her elders. Pearl, that bundle of searching intuition, is, like Hester and Dimmesdale, a projection of aspects of the author.

The world looked to Pearl much as it did to the child Nathaniel Hawthorne, who scarcely knew his father. His chaste widowed mother must have seemed to him like the virgin mother, complete within herself. Eventually seeking the father every child must have, he, like Pearl, had to search through the mother for the missing male parent. And like Pearl, he found not one man in indisputable possession, but two, one a biological father who failed to claim his wife and child, the other a man somehow related to the mother with authority of an indeterminate sort over both mother and child. This unwarranted authority was, as appears in chapter three, sufficient to separate mother and child for the sake of the boy's education—the kind of separation threatened by Governor Bellingham after Pearl's faulty response to the catechism. In Pearl's case, the true father intervened to protect the mother-child relationship from tampering by would-be surrogate fathers—a development that young Nathaniel must have wished for in vain. Viewing the action of *The Scarlet Letter* from Pearl's perspective, that of a child trying to piece together its basic family constellation, to locate its father and account for the puzzling intruder, we find her early *Umwelt* ⟨environment⟩ much like that of her creator.

When Pearl's quest is fulfilled by her father's public embrace, she gains a father only to lose him. She attains not a father's care or solicitude, only the knowledge of who her father *was*, essentially all that Hawthorne had—knowledge of a lost father. Release of Pearl's gender identity and humanity depends on acknowledgment from her biological father; her material fortunes, however, depend just as surely on the inheritance bequeathed her by Roger Chillingworth, her mother's shadowy former husband. Chillingworth endows Pearl with the means for a larger destiny than her mother alone could have supplied, and he thereby assumes a genuine aspect of the fatherly role, that of provider.

This fragmenting of the biological and the sustaining aspects of fatherhood was a critical feature of Hawthorne's childhood experience. We must imagine how he tried to construe his family constellation both before and after his father's death. Probably content at first to be the only male in the family, he suddenly found himself surrounded by Manning relatives. While still trying to discern his mother's relationship to her parents, sisters, and brothers, he found one brother, Robert Manning, taking over the affairs of all the Hawthornes. Robert Manning was generous with love, interest, and material benefits, but Nathaniel grew to resent benefactions that he felt to be intrusive coming from someone other than a father. He became excessively sensitive about dependency on the Mannings in general and on Uncle Robert in particular.

—Gloria C. Erlich, *Family Themes and Hawthorne's Fiction: The Tenacious Web* (New Brunswick, NJ: Rutgers University Press, 1984), pp. 29–30

CAROL BENSICK ON THE NOVEL OF ADULTERY

[Carol Bensick is a professor of English at the University of California at Riverside. She is the author of *La Nouvelle Beatrice: Renaissance and Romance in "Rappaccini's Daughter"* (1985). In the following essay, Bensick discusses *The Scarlet Letter* in the context of other "novels of adultery," especially two later novels, Leo Tolstoy's *Anna Karenina* (1873–77) and Gustave Flaubert's *Madame Bovary* (1857), showing how Hawthorne departs from the mainstream tradition by both depicting adultery as a violation of the moral and social order and also using adultery as a means of questioning the validity of social institutions that make extramarital sex a crime.]

"Had Hester sinned alone?" asks the narrator of *The Scarlet Letter*. Of course not; and as the literary adulteress was not alone in her "sin," so is she also not alone in her suffering. Where there is an adulteress, there must of force be a cuckold; and although the whole tradition of the novel of adultery is witness to the predictable course of his behavior, to untangle the feelings behind it was left to Hester uniquely.

Typically a man of substance and standing in his community, the literary cuckold bases his reaction to his wife's infidelity on the assumption that he can be perfectly rational about it. Indeed, the typical cuckold is accustomed to assume he is exempt from merely emotional reactions altogether. Aleksey Aleksandrovich Karenin believes that because, as he thinks, "'I am not to blame,'" it follows that, in his formulation, "'I cannot suffer.'" Almost parodying this pattern, Roger Chillingworth even convinces himself that he would proceed with tormenting Dimmesdale "'only for the art's sake.'" If this were true, Chillingworth would indeed be, as he comes to fear, a fiend. As Hawthorne portrays him, however, the cuckold is only a self-deluded man, whose mistaken belief in his own disinterested-ness sadly puts the seal on his fundamental misunderstanding with his wife.

Roger Chillingworth's successive reactions to the revelation of his wife's infidelity are clinically charted. Where Tolstoy needs to have his narrator step in to explain that Aleksey Aleksandrovich is really "profoundly miserable," we witness Chillingworth's reactions on his face. As he watches Hester from the crowd, Chillingworth's features "darken" with a "con-vulsion" of "powerful emotion." It is only "by an effort of his will" that he achieves the calm expression, finger on lips, that Hester herself sees. Although it is integral to the tragedy that Hester cannot know this, Hawthorne makes clear to us that Chillingworth has not gotten over his "horror." His feelings have only "subsided into the depths of his nature."

That the cuckold is concealing his emotions and not, as his wife thinks, failing to experience any is a crucial provision in Hawthorne's analysis of literary adultery. Anna is typical in her supposition that Aleksey Aleksandrovich is "'not a man, but a machine, and a spiteful machine,'" who simply "'doesn't care'" what she does because he "'doesn't know what love is.'" But by Chillingworth's reaction in the crowd, *The Scarlet Letter* shows that this assumption by the adulteress is a mis-take. Unhappily, it is a mistake the cuckold characteristically does everything to foster.

As *Madame Bovary* makes plain, it is in the adulteress's long-standing assumption that her husband simply lacks feel-ings that her discontent begins. But by his typical pretense to experience no emotional reaction even to infidelity, the classic cuckold effectively confirms her error; if he fails to react to *that*, then surely nothing she can do will move him. The "Recognition" scene between Hester and Chillingworth is a graphic illustration of this tragicomic pattern. Catching sight of

Chillingworth only after he has already arranged his face—missing the "convulsion" of his "horror" but getting the full offensive effect of his shushing finger—Hester, who like Anna habitually assumes that anyone who does not express feelings exactly the same way she does must not have any, is all but forced to conclude that his *only* reaction to herself, letter, and baby is a frigid concern for his good name.

Midway through *Anna Karenina*, Aleksey Aleksandrovich tells his wife that her betrayal has caused him " 'thuffering' "; without ever having him make so overt a profession, Hawthorne yet conveys Chillingworth's identical cuckold's pain. It is with a "bitter" smile that Chillingworth tells the Boston townsman, referring to Hester Prynne's husband, " 'So learned a man as you speak of should have learned this too in his books.' " In his succeeding conversation with Hester in the prison, Chillingworth betrays his suffering by fastening morbidly upon the concrete evidence of his wife's rejection: " 'The child is yours,—she is none of mine, neither will she recognize my voice or aspect as a father's.' " And through Chillingworth's revelation that he feels although " 'Elsewhere a wanderer, and isolated from human interests,' " he has now found in Boston " 'a woman, a man, a child, amongst whom and myself there exist the closest ligaments,' " Hawthorne exposes the simple cause of the classic cuckold's complicated reaction to adultery: an exclusive dependence on marriage to fill all emotional needs.

—Carol Bensick, "Demystified Adultery in *The Scarlet Letter*," *New Essays on* The Scarlet Letter, ed. Michael J. Colacurcio (Cambridge: Cambridge University Press, 1985), pp. 141–43

EVAN CARTON ON HESTER PRYNNE AS ARTIST

[Evan Carton is a professor of English at the University of Texas at Austin and the author of *Hawthorne's Transformations* (1992). In this extract from his earlier book *The Rhetoric of American Romance* (1985), Carton

discusses Hester's needlework and other artistic products as both a form of rebellion against her punishment
and as a means of uniting herself to her community.]

Through the play of what Hawthorne repeatedly calls "her art,"
Hester distinguishes Pearl and herself, indulges the "rich,
voluptuous, Oriental characteristic" in her nature, and symbolically asserts her indomitability by the social judgment and stric-
tures that have been imposed on her. Thus, again, she
metaphorically re-enacts her crime in her needlework: in "the
gorgeously beautiful, . . . the exquisite productions of her nee-
dle," she finds "a mode of expressing, and therefore soothing,
the passion of her life." Yet, if Hester's art preserves her difference, it also constitutes her bond to the Puritan community, for
it is the means by which she supports herself and Pearl and
participates in communal affairs. This dual significance, in fact,
is reflected both in the character of Hester's needlework and in
her attitude toward it. The "exquisite productions" in which she
takes "pleasure" are set against "coarse garments for the poor,"
the "rude handiwork" in which "she [offers] up a real sacrifice
of enjoyment." Taken as a whole, then, Hester's art comprises
both an expression of her passion and an internalization of its
punishment, a mode of penance.

It is not simply in her self-mortifying productions, however,
that Hester represents, rather than opposing, her society. On
the contrary, "deep ruffs, painfully wrought bands, and gorgeously embroidered gloves" are among the most fashionable
and lucrative types of her handiwork. "The taste of the age,"
Hawthorne observes, "demanding whatever was elaborate in
compositions of this kind, did not fail to extend its influence
over our stern progenitors, who had cast behind them so many
fashions which it might seem harder to dispense with." The last
clause of this sentence is the crucial one, for it obliges us to ask
why embroidery should be an indispensable indulgence for a
people that had repudiated so many others. This question and
its answer indicate Hester's most profound engagement with
the Puritan community.

Embroidery is for the Puritans what it is for Hester: an
expression of human presence, human will, human value, a
means of laying claim to the world and to oneself. Hence it is

"deemed necessary to the official state of men assuming the reins of power," is "a matter of policy" in public ceremonies, is required to "give majesty" to governmental forms, and is "demand[ed]" at funerals "to typify . . . the sorrow of the survivors." Hester's "curiously embroidered letter," then, the first product of her art, both marks her sin and her deviance and follows, even epitomizes, Puritan custom: it is, Hawthorne writes, "a specimen of . . . delicate and imaginative skill, of which the dames of a court might gladly have availed themselves, *to add the richer and more spiritual adornment of human ingenuity* to their fabrics of silk and gold" (emphasis added). More precious than the fabric of experience itself is the application of a design, the inscription of a purpose, upon it. The insistence upon such a societal inscription lies at the heart of Puritanism, as Hawthorne sees it; indeed, Puritanism depends (with magnificent literalness here) on such embroidery as Hester Prynne's. Hester practices the art of symbolic overlay by which her community gives meaning and distinction to experience, and she suffers from the symbolism that she herself purveys. Thus, her art—an art that represents not only Hester's passion but also the Puritans' social enterprise and Hawthorne's literary one—exemplifies her reality and theirs. Material fact in *The Scarlet Letter* is a matter of embroidery, of "human ingenuity" and "imaginative skill," or perhaps, as the less salutary meanings of the term would have it, of exaggeration, fabrication, specious narration.

Hester's intuition of her art's significance—of its constitutive power, its obliquity, its conduciveness to deception and even self-deception—prompts her to suspect it and to regard her pleasure in it as a sin. This is a judgment that, like the embroidery itself, implicates both Puritan reality and Hawthorne's fiction, and Hawthorne must at once acknowledge and deflect this implication. Thus the narrator contests Hester's guilty sense of her art but takes her scruples as a sign of her deviance from clarity and rectitude: "This morbid meddling of a conscience with an immaterial matter betokened . . . something doubtful, something that might be deeply wrong, beneath." Embroidery, of course, is not an "immaterial matter," and the punning play on the notion of materiality here compromises the authority of the narrator's assertion. Moreover, Hester's imposition of moral significance upon needlework exemplifies the fundamental hermeneutic principle of her society, a principle that neither she nor Hawthorne is able or willing to repudiate entirely. The paragraph that precedes the one in which Hester's judgment is criticized, in fact, suggests several moral explanations for the popularity of her needlework, explanations that assume and endorse a "morbid meddling of conscience with an immaterial matter" on the part of Hester's community. ("Vanity, it may be, chose to mortify itself, by putting on, for ceremonials of pomp and state, the garments that had been wrought by her sinful hands. . . . But it is not recorded that, in a single instance, her skill was called in aid to embroider the white veil which was to cover the pure blushes of a bride. The exception indicated the ever relentless vigor with which society frowned upon her sin.") All matters are "material" in Hester Prynne's world; as Hawthorne notes repeatedly during the opening scene of the novel, events that might be dismissed as trivial or taken up as "a theme for jest" by those in "another social state" are "invested with . . . dignity" in Puritan Boston. Yet, it is also true that no matters are material in this world, for all material facts (to paraphrase Emerson) signify (or are "invested with" the significance of) immaterial, or spiritual, facts.

—Evan Carton, "The Prison Door," *The Rhetoric of American Romance: Dialectic and Identity in Emerson, Dickinson, Poe, and Hawthorne* (Baltimore: Johns Hopkins University Press, 1985), pp. 196–99

NINA BAYM ON HESTER PRYNNE AS "OUTSIDER"

[Nina Baym (b. 1936) is a professor of English and Liberal Arts and Sciences Jubilee Professor at the University of Illinois. A leading feminist critic, she has written *The Shape of Hawthorne's Career* (1976), *Women's Fiction* (1978; rev. ed. 1993), and *Feminism and American Literary History* (1992), and is the coeditor of the fourth edition of *The Norton Anthology of American Literature* (1994). In this extract, Baym emphasizes Hester Prynne's strength of character, her individuality, and her sense of being an "outsider" in her community.]

In Hester Prynne, Hawthorne created the first true heroine of American fiction, as well as one of its enduring heroes. Hester is a heroine because she is deeply implicated in, and responsive to, the gender structure of her society, and because her story, turning on "love," is "appropriate" for a woman. She is a hero because she has qualities and actions that transcend this gender reference and lead to heroism as it can be understood for anyone.

"Such helpfulness was found in her,—so much power to do, and power to sympathize,—that many people refused to interpret the scarlet A by its original signification. They said that it meant Able; so strong was Hester Prynne, with a woman's strength." "Neither can I any longer live without her companionship; so powerful is she to sustain,—so tender to soothe!" It is impossible to miss, in these and many other passages, the stress on Hester's remarkable strength as well as the fundamentally humane uses to which she puts it. Without going beyond the license that Hawthorne allows, one might allegorize Hester as Good Power, which is, after all, precisely what, in the basic structural scheme of all narrative, one looks for in a hero. The power is remarkable in that its existence seems so improbable in an outcast woman. If the Puritan state draws its power from the consensual community and the laws that uphold it, then clearly Hester has access to a completely different source of power—or is, perhaps, herself an alternative source of power. And it is a power that even the Puritan world cannot deny, for "with her native energy of character, and rare capacity, it could not entirely cast her off."

Perhaps, however, it is precisely her essential alienation from the community that explains this power. Although Hester can hardly doubt the power of the Puritan community to punish her and define the circumstances of her life, she knows—as we do—that they have this power only because she has granted it to them. She is free to leave Boston whenever she chooses. Her decision to stay entails a submission to Puritan power, but since she can withdraw her consent at any time this submission is always provisional. Her reasons for staying may be misguided, but they are her own. In schematic terms, if the Puritans symbolize the law, then Hester symbolizes the individual person—with this important proviso: she also symbolizes good. It would be easy to deduce from this polarity that Hawthorne wants us to think that law is bad and the individual good—but that would be too easy. Matters in Hawthorne are never so clear-cut. But he certainly gives us a situation wherein two kinds of power confront each other in conflict, and strongly suggests that any society that regards the power of the individual only as an adversary to be overcome, is profoundly defective and deeply inhuman.

Hester's situation, even before the commission of her "sin," is that of an outsider. She was sent to Massachusetts in advance of her husband; he had decided to emigrate, not she. The native strength of her character is certainly abetted by the fact that, as a young woman in a society dominated by aging men, she has no public importance. Even when she becomes a public figure through her punishment, her psyche is largely left alone. The magistrates condemn her to wear the letter but thereafter seem to have only a very superficial interest in her. A minister who sees her on the street may take the opportunity to preach an extempore sermon; people stare at the letter; children jeer; but none of this behavior represents an attempt to change Hester's mind. It is hoped that the external letter will work its way down into Hester's heart and cause repentance, but nobody really cares and this indifference is Hester's freedom. In fact, the effect of the letter so far as Hester's character is concerned is the opposite of what was intended: turning her into a public symbol, it conceals her individuality and thus protects it.

As the representative of individuality, Hester, rather than subjecting herself to the law, subjects it to her own scrutiny; as I have said, she takes herself as a law. She is not, by nature, rebellious; and during the seven-year period of *The Scarlet Letter*'s action, she certainly attempts to accept the judgment implicit in the letter. If she could accept that judgment she would be able to see purpose and meaning in her suffering. But ultimately she is unable to transcend her heartfelt conviction that she has not sinned. She loves Dimmesdale, with whom she sinned; she loves the child that her sin brought forth. How, then, can she agree that her deed was wrong?

She goes so far in her thinking as to attribute her own law to God, thus denying the entire rationale of the Puritan community, their certainty that their laws conform to divine intention. "Man had marked this woman's sin by a scarlet letter, which had such potent and disastrous efficacy that no human sympathy could reach her, save it were sinful like herself. God, as a direct consequence of the sin which man thus punished, had given her a lovely child, whose place was on that same dishonored bosom, to connect her parent for ever with the race and descent of mortals, and to be finally a blessed soul in heaven!"
—Nina Baym, "Who? The Characters," The Scarlet Letter: *A Reading* (Boston: Twayne, 1986), pp. 62–64

KENNETH MARC HARRIS ON HESTER PRYNNE'S SEXUALITY

[Kenneth Marc Harris is Lecturer in American Studies at the University of Canterbury in Christchurch, New Zealand. He has written *Carlyle and Emerson: Their Long Debate* (1978) and *The Film Fetish* (1992), in addition to a book on Hawthorne from which the following extract is taken. Here Harris discusses the emergence of Hester's sexuality and sees in it a symbol for her metaphorical escape from the narrowness of Puritan society and for her renewed will to live.]

Hester is saved—by which I mean she renews her love of life and her faith in humankind—when she ceases to be a hypocrite and reaffirms her true identity. The transformation is at first symbolic, then literal. When Dimmesdale refuses to forgive her for not warning him about Chillingworth, she impulsively presses "his head against her bosom; little caring though his cheek rested on the scarlet letter." This is the same bosom that for seven years has served as a soft but affectionless pillow for heads whose owners she didn't care about; it has been utilized, to be more explicit, as part of a revenge-inspired strategy to change the public perception of the emblem that is attached to it. Now her bosom is suddenly, almost miraculously restored—with "sudden and desperate tenderness"—to its function as a source and center of natural human passion, regardless of whatever labels a hypocritical society may choose to affix to it. As she holds Dimmesdale to her breast despite his vain efforts to break free, she can appreciate the difference between feeling a kindly regard for his prosperity and reputation—all she once thought she was concerned about—and loving him, even against his will, smothering him with her love, as it were. Yet the nurturing quality of her outburst of passion is attested to by Dimmesdale, who shortly after being so roughly womanhandled says to himself: "So powerful is she to sustain,—so tender to soothe!"

The symbolic restoration of feminine virtue to her breast is paralleled by the equally instantaneous restoration of her physical sexuality. In a gorgeous paragraph her hypocritical pseudo–nun's habit, given in synecdoche as "the formal cap that confined her hair," is removed to reveal the long-repressed woman within. In a virtuoso exhibition of female sexual imagery, the dark, abundant hair falls down her shoulders to create a chiaroscuro effect, "imparting the charm of softness to her features"; a playful, Mona Lisa smile "that seemed gushing from the very heart of womanhood" lights up her face; and a "crimson flush" is set to "glowing on her cheek, that had been long so pale." A race of hypocrites, afraid of their own sexuality and jealous of hers, had turned her into an asexual idol, and she, to her peril, had participated in her own dehumanization, but now, by another semi-miraculous "impulse" she has called back her true self from seeming oblivion. "Her sex, her youth, and the whole richness of her beauty, came back from what men call the irrevocable past," and the sky, the trees, and the little brook, availing themselves of the pathetic fallacy, exuberantly join in the celebration of her rebirth.

The next time we see Hester in her sister of mercy costume, as she waits for Dimmesdale to wrap up his affairs so they can decamp, she is no longer a self-deceiving hypocrite but rather a conscious dissembler, a trickster. In fact, she is actually impersonating her previous, phony self: her face is "like a mask" in that it is designed to mislead others, not herself any longer. Behind it the reborn sensual woman is thinking: "Look your last on the scarlet letter and its wearer!" At the same time, the narrator adds—rather apologetically, almost defensively—that she had some "feeling of regret" at leaving, which I take not so much as a moral foreshadowing of her failure to escape but more as a suspense-building device, because Hawthorne knows that at this point we are on her side (if only temporarily) even though we recognize that her arguments to Dimmesdale that running off with her is the morally right thing to do are blatantly self-serving. We can infer from his uncharacteristically assertive (and embarrassed) "Hush, Hester!" that Dimmesdale, like the reader, sees through her self-deceiving assurance that their adultery "had a consecration of its own." She deceives herself in this regard so easily, almost (but not quite) innocently, because after seven years of isolated freethinking the Ten Commandments simply don't have quite the moral import with her that they still carry for him. That is why in the final analysis their failure to escape is a part of his story, not hers. Mentally, she has already left. Or to put it another way, they fail to escape because escape is an impossibility for him, not for her—except, of course, to the extent that escape *without him* is impossible for her, which was really why she hadn't gone away by herself in the first place notwithstanding her self-deceiving rationale about working out her penance. The impossibility of her escaping without him also seems to be the main reason she comes back after his death. Had he died in Europe, she certainly would have stayed there. All the same, her having fallen in love with Dimmesdale was no accident: in other words, we shouldn't attribute her failure to find happiness and fulfillment in Europe with the man she loves entirely to her rotten luck in loving a man who lacked the audacity to throw off his old habits of thinking. His lack of courage, after all—his vulnerability—was precisely what attracted her to him, along with his repressed sensuality. The reason he disappoints her, then, is the very reason for which she chose him.

Her sexuality had been long repressed too, which was why she had once thought she could tolerate life with the misshapen Chillingworth, an illusion she might well have continued to entertain had not the affair with Dimmesdale showed her otherwise. Fear of sexuality entails a fear of life, and after again damming up her sexuality following her disgrace, her fear of life moved to the forefront of her mind in the form of a death wish. Once more an encounter with Dimmesdale revitalized her. But his death did not lead to further repression: there was no longer a need to repress her libido, since the only man who could satisfy it was gone. Yet the continued healthiness of her sexuality in her later years is evident from her effectiveness as counselor and consoler of women with amatory complaints. She can help others to learn to enjoy their lives because she overcame forever her fear of her own life.

> —Kenneth Marc Harris, *Hypocrisy and Self-Deception in Hawthorne's Fiction* (Charlottesville: University Press of Virginia, 1988), pp. 64–66

DAVID S. REYNOLDS ON HESTER PRYNNE AS A "FALLEN WOMAN"

[David S. Reynolds (b. 1948), formerly a professor of English at Rutgers University, is the author of *Faith in Fiction: The Emergence of Religious Literature in America* (1981) and a critical study of the nineteenth-century American author George Lippard (1982). In this extract, Reynolds places Hawthorne's novel in the context of the popular literature of its time, noting how Hester Prynne is a radically transformed version of the "fallen woman" of the conventional novels of the day.]

Although Hawthorne is generally credited with having created the most intriguing heroines in pre–Civil War literature, little has been said about the relationship between these heroines and the women's culture of the day. The fact is that the rich variety of female character types in antebellum popular culture prepared the way for Hawthorne's complex heroines. Hawthorne's best fiction occupies an energetic middle space between the Conventional novel and the literature of women's

wrongs. Skeptical of the Conventional and politically un-
committed, Hawthorne was in an ideal position to choose
judiciously from the numerous female stereotypes and to
assimilate them in literary texts. His career illustrates the success of an especially responsive author in gathering together
disparate female types and recombining them artistically so
that they became crucial elements of the rhetorical and artistic
construct of his fiction. ⟨. . .⟩

She is, in short, the quintessential American heroine, reflecting virtually every facet of the antebellum woman's experience.
As was true with Beatrice Rappaccini, the innovative fusion of
contrasting stereotypes creates a wholly new kind of heroine
who bears little resemblance to any individual popular character. The fusion serves specific rhetorical functions for
Hawthorne. The gathering together of different female types in
Hester Prynne is an assertion of unity in the face of a fragmentation of women's roles that Hawthorne perceived in his contemporary culture. It was precisely this fragmentation of roles
that would produce an indirect, elliptical style among some
American women writers of the 1850s and 1860s. Through a
majestic act of artistry, Hawthorne temporarily fends off the
potential confusion inherent in shifting women's roles by creating a heroine who is magically able to act out several of these
roles simultaneously.

What makes possible this complex heroine is Hawthorne's
adept use of the Puritan past. Just as Puritanism added moral
depth to sensational themes that had degenerated in popular
literature into flat prurience, so it offered historical materials
conducive to a serious, rounded treatment of women's issues
that had become sensationalized in popular Subversive fiction
and circumvented in Conventional fiction. In *The Scarlet Letter*
Hawthorne not only adopts but also *transforms* popular female
stereotypes, and the chief transforming agent is Puritanism. The
sympathetic fallen woman, who in radical-democrat novels had
led to a gleeful inversion of moral values, here is treated with
high seriousness. We sympathize with Hester but, because of
the enormity of her punishment (a punishment reflecting the
moral severity of Puritan New England), we are impressed with
the momentousness of her sin. That is to say, she is not the fall-
en woman of the antebellum sensational novel who becomes

callously amoral or vindictively murderous. Similarly, she is not the typical working woman, one who either gives way to suicidal despair, or becomes a prostitute, or contemplates armed revolution. Hawthorne knew well the plight of American seamstresses, and in the novel he points out that needlework was "then, as now, almost the only one within a woman's grasp." But instead of emphasizing the degradation accompanying woman's work, he transforms this work into a triumphant assertion of woman's artistic power, as evidenced by the intricate, superb patterns Hester produces. The sensual woman, who in pamphlet novels of the 1840s was an insatiable nymphomaniac demanding many sexual partners, is here changed into a passionate but restrained woman who worships the sexual act with just one partner and whose dream of escaping with her lover is carefully squelched by Hawthorne.

The feminist exemplar is another popular stereotype Hawthorne transforms. At key points in the novel we are told that Hester broods over women's wrongs and dreams of a total change in male-female relations. But she never agitates publicly for women's rights, and it is clear by the end of the novel that Hawthorne has in mind not a militant, angry feminism but rather a gradualist moral exemplar feminism with utopian overtones. As a counselor of troubled women, the aged Hester assures them that "at some brighter period, when the world shall have grown ripe for it, in Heaven's own time, a new truth would be revealed, in order to establish the whole relation between man and woman on a surer ground of mutual happiness." Not only is the feminist revolution delayed to a vague, ideal future, but also Hester discounts her own capacities as a feminist exemplar by stressing that "the angel and apostle of the coming revelation must be a woman, indeed, but lofty, pure, and beautiful" and wise "not through dusky grief, but the ethereal medium of joy."

Hawthorne, therefore, attempts in *The Scarlet Letter* to absorb his culture's darkest, most disturbing female stereotypes and to rescue them from prurience or noisy politics by reinterpreting them in terms of bygone Puritanism and by fusing them with the moral exemplar. Evidently, his attempted brightening of dark stereotypes through the character of Hester was not altogether successful for either Hawthorne or his wife.

Hawthorne lamented what he described as the unrelieved gloom of *The Scarlet Letter,* which he hoped would be published in a volume that would also contain more cheerful tales. As for his wife, after reading the novel she reportedly went to bed with a throbbing headache. He had created a magnificent fusion of different character types in Hester but had in the process sacrificed clear meaning. If he and Sophia were puzzled whether Beatrice Rappaccini was an angel or a demon, they had reason to be even more puzzled over Hester. To this day, critics still argue over the degree to which Hawthorne sympathizes with his most famous heroine. Actually, as was true with Beatrice, no absolute meaning or distinct authorial attitude can be gleaned from the complicated Hester. He recognized the disparate female types in his contemporary culture and created in Hester Prynne a multifaceted heroine in whom these types were artistically fused.

> —David S. Reynolds, "Toward Hester Prynne," *Beneath the American Renaissance: The Subversive Imagination in the Age of Emerson and Melville* (New York: Knopf, 1988), pp. 368, 373–75

[Edwin Haviland Miller (b. 1918) is a former professor of English at New York University and a distinguished critic and biographer. Among his works are *The Professional Writer in Elizabethan England* (1959) and *Walt Whitman's Poetry: A Psychological Study* (1969). Miller has also edited several works by Whitman and written a biography of Herman Melville (1975). In this extract, taken from his exhaustive new biography of Hawthorne (1991), Miller shows how each major character in *The Scarlet Letter* reflects some facet of Hawthorne's own personality.]

While the four characters have separate identities, collectively they constitute a subtle and complex self-portrait, Hawthorne being the sum total of all his characters. Each is an artist: Hester in embroidery, Dimmesdale in the outpourings of the tongue of flames, Chillingworth in his concoctions for body and soul, and Pearl in her fashionings of natural objects. Like artists they brood over and live in the "interior kingdom." Hester transcends a hostile world, first, by her quiet dedication to the public good and, second, by her speculation as to the nature of the patriarchal world and a future society which will "establish the whole relation between man and woman on a surer ground of mutual happiness." Dimmesdale's "constant introspection" stems not so much from guilt because of his "sin" as from his inability to establish loving connections because of the self-love and egomania which stem from insecurities and fright. Chillingworth is "a man chiefly accustomed to look inward, and to whom external matters are of little value and import, unless they bear relation to something within his mind." Pearl's "inner world" seethes with her repressed rage as an isolated child in a hostile environment: "The singularity lay in the hostile feelings with which the child regarded all these offsprings of her own heart and mind. She never created a friend, but seemed always to be sowing broadcast the dragon's teeth, whence sprung a harvest of armed enemies, against whom she rushed to battle." Because Pearl seems to originate in allegory or in the myth of Cadmus, we as readers forget that her deprivations are Hawthorne's: he too understood what it meant to be fatherless.

In delineating the characters, Hawthorne has drawn upon his own mirror image. Pearl may recall Una Hawthorne as many have suggested or his sister Elizabeth, as a recent commentator has proposed, but one suspects she is essentially a portrait of Hawthorne as a child, with "a beauty that shone with deep and vivid tints; a bright complexion, eyes possessing intensity both of depth and glow, and hair already of a deep, glossy brown." Dimmesdale mirrors Hawthorne's physical appearance and the indecisive, conflicted part of his nature.

> He was a person of very striking aspect, with a white lofty, and impending brow, large, brown, melancholy eyes, and a mouth which, unless when he forcibly compressed it, was apt to be tremulous, expressing both nervous sensibility and a vast power of self-restraint. [There was] a startled, a half-frightened look,— as of a being who felt himself quite astray and at a loss in the pathway of human existence, and could only be at ease in some seclusion of his own.

Roger Chillingworth, eyes spurting fire, like one of the Gorgons, would seem to originate in the gothic and the unconscious monsterland of dreams and nightmares. But he walks with one shoulder raised, like Hawthorne himself, and familially he is the descendant of those two Hathorne men of iron whom the heir feared and revered. Chillingworth also shares with the author the roles of Paul Pry or voyeur and analyst of psychosomatic disturbances. (Some claim that he is fiction's first psychoanalyst.) Although Chillingworth plays the role of cuckold and villain—and Hawthorne poses the questions as to who is the greater sinner, the deceitful, hypocritical clergyman or the duplicitous doctor—it is perhaps closer to the truth, and reality, to observe that Chillingworth is the sadistic side of Dimmesdale's masochism.

> —Edwin Haviland Miller, *Salem Is My Dwelling Place: A Life of Nathaniel Hawthorne* (Iowa City: University of Iowa Press, 1991), pp. 296–97

CHARLES SWANN ON HESTER PRYNNE AND THE PATRIARCHAL SOCIETY

[Charles Swann is a professor of English at the University of Keele, England. In this extract, Swann shows how Hester Prynne both defies and unconsciously acquiesces in the dictates of her patriarchal society.]

For such a short fiction, *The Scarlet Letter* covers a remarkable length of time—and a period which has a considerable historical resonance: seven years—1642–49. Whatever the reason for choosing the period of England's Civil War for the main action of the novel, a substantial length of time is necessary for Hester to build a new identity after her old European self had been destroyed by her sin and its punishment on the scaffold: "It was as if a new birth, with stronger assimilations than the first, had converted the forest-land . . . into Hester Prynne's . . . lifelong home." And not only Hester's construction of a new self but also the related matter of the mutual relationships between herself and the community have to be given time to develop so that a long revolution in the community's interpretation of the letter and Hester can take place. That relationship is not only long but complex—and not without its ironies. One irony is that her subversion by decoration of the letter not only enables Hester to find a place in the community's economy but also that art of needlework, that labour of the outsider, in large part reinforces the power structure of the society—even though her own thoughts radically question that structure:

> Public ceremonies, such as ordinations, the installation of magis-trates, and all that could give majesty to the forms in which a new government manifested itself to the people, were, as a matter of policy, marked by a stately and well-conducted cere-monial, and a sombre but yet a studied magnificence. Deep ruffs, painfully wrought bands, and gorgeously embroidered gloves, were all deemed necessary to the official state of men assuming the reins of power; and were readily allowed to indi-viduals dignified by rank or wealth, even while sumptuary laws forbade these and similar extravagances to the plebeian order.

There is much that could be said about this passage—but one obvious point is that Hawthorne is drawing attention to the class structure of the infant democracy. In so far as her identity is constituted by the letter signifying one meaning along with her labour for the establishment, the patriarchy could hardly ask for a more useful "citizen" than Hester—at once a strong warning against hiding the father who has bro-ken the rules and a figure who enables the patriarchy (both fathers in Christ and fathers in the law) symbolically to declare their command over "painfully wrought" labour—a labour which in its products signifies their power, their difference from "the plebeian order." But the simplicity of symbolic labelling cannot, over time, survive the necessary multiplicity of Hester's relationships with the society as a whole. For example, not all Hester's labour (if all her paid work) goes towards making the symbols of power: she uses the profit ("all her superfluous means") to make "coarse garments for the poor." Though that activity certainly reflects and by reflecting may endorse class difference within the society, it is also a response to need—and in that response a beginning to her social work as well as pri-

vate penance (remorse for past sins, in its technical meaning—
but not, significantly, yet penitence—technically the resolve to
sin no more).

> —Charles Swann, "*The Scarlet Letter* and the Language of
> History," *Nathaniel Hawthorne: Tradition and Revolution*
> (Cambridge: Cambridge University Press, 1991), pp. 87–88

Books by
Nathaniel Hawthorne

Fanshawe: A Tale. 1828.

Twice-Told Tales. 1837, 1842 (2 vols.).

Peter Parley's Universal History (editor; with Elizabeth Hawthorne). 1837. 2 vols.

Time's Portraiture: Being the Carrier's Address to the Patrons of the Salem Gazette *for the First of January, 1838.* 1838.

The Sister Years: Being the Carrier's Address to the Patrons of the Salem Gazette *for the First of January, 1839.* 1839.

Grandfather's Chair: A History for Youth. 1841.

Famous Old People: Being the Second Epoch of Grandfather's Chair. 1841.

Liberty Tree, with the Last Words of Grandfather's Chair. 1841.

Biographical Stories for Children. 1842.

The Celestial Rail-road. 1843.

Journal of an African Cruiser by Horatio Bridge (editor). 1845.

Mosses from an Old Manse. 1846. 2 vols.

The Scarlet Letter: A Romance. 1850.

The House of the Seven Gables: A Romance. 1851.

A Wonder-Book for Girls and Boys. 1852.

The Snow-Image and Other Twice-Told Tales. 1852.

The Blithedale Romance. 1852.

Life of Franklin Pierce. 1852.

Tanglewood Tales for Girls and Boys: Being a Second Wonder-Book. 1853.

The Marble Faun; or, The Romance of Monte Beni. 1860. 2 vols.

Our Old Home: A Series of English Sketches. 1863.

Pansie, A Fragment: The Last Literary Effort of Nathaniel Hawthorne. 1864.

Passages from the American Note-books. Ed. Sophia Hawthorne. 1868. 2 vols.

Passages from the English Note-books. Ed. Sophia Hawthorne. 1870. 2 vols.

Passages from the French and Italian Note-books. Ed. Una Hawthorne. 1871. 2 vols.

Septimius Felton; or, The Elixir of Life. Ed. Una Hawthorne and Robert Browning. 1872.

The Dolliver Romance and Other Pieces. Ed. Sophia Hawthorne. 1876.

Doctor Grimshawe's Secret: A Romance. Ed. Julian Hawthorne. 1883.

Works (Riverside Edition). Ed. George Parsons Lathrop. 1883. 12 vols.

Complete Writings (Autograph Edition). 1900. 22 vols.

Twenty Days with Julian and Little Bunny: A Diary. 1904.

Love Letters. 1907. 2 vols.

Letters to William D. Ticknor. 1910. 2 vols.

Works. Ed. Charles Curtis Bigelow. 1923. 10 vols.

The Heart of Hawthorne's Journals. Ed. Newton Arvin. 1929.

Complete Novels and Selected Tales. Ed. Norman Holmes Pearson. 1937.

Hawthorne as Editor: Selections from his Writings in the American Magazine of Useful and Entertaining Knowledge. Ed. Arlin Turner. 1941.

Works (Centenary Edition). Ed. William Charvat et al. 1962–88.
 20 vols.

Hawthorne's Lost Notebook 1835–1841. Ed. Barbara S.
 Mouffe. 1978.

Travel Sketches. Ed. Alfred Weber, Beth L. Lueck, and Dennis
 Berthold. 1989.

Works about
Nathaniel Hawthorne and
The Scarlet Letter

Abel, Darrel. *The Moral Picturesque: Studies in Hawthorne's Fiction.* West Lafayette, IN: Purdue University Press, 1988.

Arvin, Newton. *Hawthorne.* Boston: Little, Brown, 1929.

Baskett, Sam S. "*The* (Complete) *Scarlet Letter.*" *College English* 22 (1961): 321–28.

Baym, Nina. *The Shape of Hawthorne's Career.* Ithaca, NY: Cornell University Press, 1976.

Becker, John E. *Hawthorne's Historical Allegory: An Examination of the American Conscience.* Port Washington, NY: Kennikat Press, 1971.

Bell, Millicent. *Hawthorne's View of the Artist.* Albany: State University of New York Press, 1962.

Bercovitch, Sacvan. *The Office of* The Scarlet Letter. Baltimore: Johns Hopkins University Press, 1991.

Berlant, Lauren. *The Anatomy of National Fantasy: Hawthorne, Utopia, and Everyday Life.* Chicago: University of Chicago Press, 1991.

Bloom, Harold, ed. *Hester Prynne.* New York: Chelsea House, 1990.

————, ed. *Nathaniel Hawthorne's* The Scarlet Letter. New York: Chelsea House, 1986.

Brodhead, Richard H. *The School of Hawthorne.* New York: Oxford University Press, 1986.

Browning, Preston M., Jr. "Hester Prynne as a Secular Saint." *Midwest Quarterly* 13 (1972): 351–62.

Budick, Emily Miller. *Engendering Romance: Women Writers and the Hawthorne Tradition 1850–1900.* New Haven: Yale University Press, 1994.

Charvat, William; Pearce, Roy Harvey; and Simpson, Claude M., ed. *Hawthorne Centenary Essays.* Columbus: Ohio State University Press, 1964.

Colacurcio, Michael J. "Footsteps of Ann Hutchinson: The Context of *The Scarlet Letter.*" *ELH* 39 (1972): 459–94.

Cox, James M. "*The Scarlet Letter:* Through the Old Manse and the Custom House." *Virginia Quarterly Review* 51 (1975): 432–47.

Crews, Frederick C. *The Sins of the Fathers: Hawthorne's Psychological Themes.* New York: Oxford University Press, 1966.

Darnell, Donald. "*The Scarlet Letter:* Hawthorne's Emblem Book." *Studies in American Fiction* 7 (1979): 153–62.

Dauber, Kenneth. *Rediscovering Hawthorne.* Princeton: Princeton University Press, 1977.

DeSalvo, Louise. *Nathaniel Hawthorne.* Atlantic Highlands, NJ: Humanities Press, 1987.

Donohue, Agnes McNeill. *Hawthorne: Calvin's Ironic Stepchild.* Kent, OH: Kent State University Press, 1985.

Elder, Marjorie J. *Nathaniel Hawthorne: Transcendental Symbolist.* Athens: Ohio University Press, 1969.

Fogle, Richard Harter. *Hawthorne's Fiction: The Light and the Dark.* Rev. ed. Norman: University of Oklahoma Press, 1964.

Gale, Robert L. *A Nathaniel Hawthorne Encyclopedia.* Westport, CT: Greenwood Press, 1988.

Gerber, John C., ed. *Twentieth Century Interpretations of* The Scarlet Letter. Englewood Cliffs, NJ: Prentice-Hall, 1968.

Greiner, Donald J. *Adultery in the American Novel: Updike, James, and Hawthorne.* Columbia: University of South Carolina Press, 1985.

Houston, Neal Bryan. "Hester Prynne as Eternal Feminine." *Discourse* 9 (1966): 230–44.

Hutner, Gordon. *Secrets and Sympathy: Forms of Disclosure in Hawthorne's Novels.* Athens: University of Georgia Press, 1988.

Jacobsen, Richard J. *Hawthorne's Conception of the Creative Process.* Cambridge, MA: Harvard University Press, 1965.

Katz, Seymour. " 'Character,' 'Nature,' and Allegory in *The Scarlet Letter.*" *Nineteenth-Century Fiction* 23 (1968–69): 3–17.

Lee, A. Robert, ed. *Nathaniel Hawthorne: New Critical Essays.* Totowa, NJ: Barnes & Noble, 1982.

Leverenz, David. "Mrs. Hawthorne's Headache: Reading *The Scarlet Letter.*" *Nineteenth-Century Fiction* 37 (1982–83): 552–75.

Levin, Harry. *The Power of Blackness: Hawthorne, Poe, Melville.* New York: Alfred A. Knopf, 1958.

Lewis, R. W. B. "The Return into Time: Hawthorne." In *The American Adam: Innocence, Tragedy and Tradition in the Nineteenth Century.* Chicago: University of Chicago Press, 1955, pp. 110–26.

Lloyd-Smith, Allan Gardner. *Eve Tempted: Writing and Sexuality in Hawthorne's Fiction.* Totowa, NJ: Barnes & Noble, 1983.

McWilliams, John P., Jr. *Hawthorne, Melville, and the American Character: A Looking-Glass Business.* Cambridge: Cambridge University Press, 1984.

Male, Roy R. *Hawthorne's Tragic Vision.* Austin: University of Texas Press, 1957.

Martin, Terence. *Nathaniel Hawthorne.* Rev. ed. Boston: Twayne, 1983.

Mellow, James R. *Nathaniel Hawthorne in His Times.* Boston: Houghton Mifflin, 1980.

Miller, J. Hillis. *Hawthorne and History: Defacing It.* Cambridge, MA: Basil Blackwell, 1991.

Millington, Richard H. *Practicing Romance: Narrative Form and Cultural Engagement in Hawthorne's Fiction.* Princeton: Princeton University Press, 1992.

Normand, Jean. *Nathaniel Hawthorne: An Approach to an Analysis of Artistic Creation.* Tr. Derek Coltman. Cleveland: Press of Case Western Reserve University, 1970.

Ragussis, Michael. "Family Discourse and Fiction in *The Scarlet Letter.*" *ELH* 49 (1982): 863–88.

Reid, Alfred S. *The Yellow Ruff and* The Scarlet Letter: *A Source of Hawthorne's Novel.* Gainesville: University of Florida Press, 1955.

Reynolds, Larry J. "*The Scarlet Letter* and Revolutions Abroad." *American Literature* 57 (1985): 44–67.

Rosa, Alfred. *Salem, Transcendentalism, and Hawthorne.* Rutherford, NJ: Fairleigh Dickinson University Press, 1980.

Sarracino, Carmine. "*The Scarlet Letter* and a New Ethic." *College Literature* 10 (1983): 50–59.

Scharnhorst, Gary, ed. *The Critical Response to Nathaniel Hawthorne's* The Scarlet Letter. Westport, CT: Greenwood Press, 1992.

Stubbs, John C. *The Pursuit of Form: A Study of Hawthorne and the Romance.* Urbana: University of Illinois Press, 1970.

Turner, Arlin. *Nathaniel Hawthorne: A Biography.* New York: Oxford University Press, 1980.

Wagenknecht, Edward. *Nathaniel Hawthorne: Man and Writer.* New York: Oxford University Press, 1961.

———. *Nathaniel Hawthorne: The Man, His Tales, and Romances.* New York: Frederick Ungar Publishing Co., 1989.

Waggoner, Hyatt H. *Hawthorne: A Critical Study.* Cambridge, MA: Harvard University Press, 1955.

Index of
Themes and Ideas